Every Day with Jesus

with Jesus

SEP/OCT 2020

Deeply Rooted

'blessed is the one who trusts in the LORD... They will
be like a tree... that sends out its roots by the stream.'
Jeremiah 17:7–8

Selwyn Hughes
Revised and updated by Mick Brooks

© CWR 2020. Dated text previously published as *Roots That Go Down Deep* (Sep/Oct 2005) by CWR. This edition revised and updated for 2020 by Mick Brooks.

CWR, Waverley Abbey House, Waverley Lane, Farnham, Surrey GU9 8EP, UK **Tel: 01252 784700**
Email: mail@cwr.org.uk Registered Charity No. 294387. Registered Limited Company No. 1990308.

Cover image: Stocksy.com/Cosma Andrei
Quiet Time image: Adobe Stock
Printed in England by Linney

MIX
Paper from
responsible sources
FSC® C015900

A word of introduction...

I have no doubt that many of you receiving this issue will have at the forefront of your minds the impact that the COVID-19 pandemic has had, and in many ways continues to have on us all. With much of the world facing unprecedented changes to our daily lives and routines, Waverley Abbey House (CWR's home base) had to close its doors for the first time since 1987. I hope that, as you read this, we are emerging on the other side – and that those of us who may have been personally impacted and affected can draw comfort knowing that Jesus has promised to not leave us and has promised His presence to us.

It's been remarkable to see how so many of the things we take for granted can quickly unravel. But, by God's grace, despite many staff having been furloughed and the financial challenges faced by the ministry at this time, this issue of *Every Day with Jesus* has still made it into your hands as we celebrate 55 years of its publication. In these pages, Selwyn unpacks how we can put down strong spiritual roots so that in times of drought and difficulty we can stand firm, and not just survive but thrive. Jesus, who knew of this world's struggles, prepared a way for us to put down roots in Him which will anchor us when the ground beneath us shifts. What fitting thoughts for such a time as this. My prayer is that these devotions will deepen and strengthen your spiritual roots and enrich you as you draw life from the source of life itself – our heavenly Father.

God bless,

Mick Brooks, Consulting Editor

Free small group resource to accompany this issue can be found at
cwr.org.uk/extra

f The *EDWJ* Facebook community is growing!
To join the conversation visit **facebook.com/edwjpage**

Deeply rooted

FOR READING & MEDITATION – JEREMIAH 17:5–8

*'blessed is the one who trusts in the Lord... They will be like a tree...
that sends out its roots by the stream.' (vv7–8)*

The theme for this issue, Deeply Rooted, came to me while I was reading about a visit to a vineyard in the Napa Valley, California. The visitor to the vineyard had been told that the tap roots of some vines can go down as much as 40 feet to reach the water table. As the thought of these roots going down so deep so that the vines might bear fruit lingered in my mind, the Holy Spirit seemed to whisper, 'Write for me on this theme.'

One of the most important reasons for producing *Every Day with Jesus* is to help Christians put down spiritual roots instead of relying on others to provide their spiritual nourishment. A Christian can develop roots that go down deep into God through daily meditation on His Word, through prayer, and by depending on the Holy Spirit. When I say a Christian can develop roots, I am not suggesting the Christian life is a matter of self-effort. I am simply saying there are certain things we can do, and if we are not intentional then we will become, in Jeremiah's words, 'like a bush in the wastelands' (v6). Christian maturity is not accidental – it takes place when we draw on the resources God has provided.

FURTHER STUDY

Isa. 37:31;
Luke 8:4–15

1. How can we become fruitful Christians?

2. What caused the plants to wither?

God's will is that we should live fruitful lives, and that fruit is produced to the extent that, like the vines we have mentioned, we encourage our roots to grow – roots that draw nourishment from a close relationship with and a daily dependence on the God who can be trusted. If our spiritual roots draw only from the surface waters of life's circumstances, fruitfulness is hard to sustain. Mark it and mark it well: the more deeply our roots go down, the more fruitful our lives above ground.

God my Father, please help me see any steps I need to take in order to send my spiritual roots down deeper into You. Help me draw not from the surface waters of life but from the deep springs found in You. In Jesus' name I pray. Amen.

'We are what we respond to'

FOR READING & MEDITATION – HEBREWS 2:1–13

'how shall we escape if we ignore so great a salvation?' (v3)

Yesterday we said that Christian maturity is not accidental; it occurs as we draw on all the resources God has provided for us. You may have heard it said: 'We are what we respond to, nothing more and nothing less.' A Christian has been described as someone who responds to all the discoveries he or she makes in their developing relationship with Christ. It's important for us, then, to respond to Jesus. When we do, we will find that we discover even more. Though God enables us to grow in our Christian life, we have a part to play too. Our calling is to respond to all that He reveals to us of Himself. Let's move beyond the idea that all we need to do is to sit back and let God act in our lives. To fully take hold of all of the divine resources available involves developing spiritual habits and cultivating spiritual practices.

FURTHER STUDY

2 Pet. 1:1–11

1. What has God given to us?
2. How should we respond?

In the book of Acts we read this about the early Christians: 'They devoted themselves to the apostles' teaching and to fellowship, to the breaking of bread and to prayer' (Acts 2:42). Notice the words 'they devoted themselves'. If conversion is the beginning of God's work within us, then cultivation of that work follows on (see Phil. 1:6; 2:12–13).

Many Christians start well, but soon the initial enthusiasm fades and they settle for respectable mediocrity, mostly because we fail to draw on the resources of God. We quickly revert to self-reliance. The Authorised Version of today's text reads, 'How shall we escape, if we neglect so great salvation?' The Christian life may become impoverished, not because of a sinful lifestyle, but because we have not put in place a few basic practices that would help encourage the growth of our spiritual roots.

Father, forgive me if I am not cultivating and tending my spiritual roots so that they go deeper into You. I want not just enough to live on, but enough also to spare. Help me be a Christian who overflows with godliness. In Jesus' name. Amen.

Cultivating the soul

FOR READING & MEDITATION – GENESIS 2:4–15

'The LORD God took the man and put him in the Garden of Eden to work it and take care of it.' (v15)

Thomas Moore, whose book *Care of the Soul* struck a nerve among Christians in the USA, said, 'Everyone should know that you can't live in any other way than by cultivating the soul.'

I have used the following illustration before, but it bears repeating. A certain man was showing his friend around his beautiful garden, on which he had lavished years of attention. Once it had been a wilderness with no shape or colour, but years of hard work had turned it into a delightful place. 'This is indeed a beautiful garden,' the friend said. 'How God should be praised for such handiwork.' The owner of the garden hesitated and then said, 'Yes, God most certainly should be praised, but you should have seen it when He had it all to Himself!' This man was not being irreverent but highlighting that though God is the creator, human beings need to care for what He has made because the Fall has marred His creation.

FURTHER STUDY

Psa. 128:1–6; Prov. 24:30–34

1. What happens when we walk in God's ways?

2. What was learned from the field of the sluggard?

It is said that John Wesley, the founder of Methodism, rode a total of 250,000 miles on horseback during the years of his ministry. Often he preached ten times a week. In addition, he spent a considerable amount of time dealing with his correspondence. John Wesley was one of the most time-pressured yet influential Christians who has ever lived. Why was he so fruitful? He was fruitful because he learned the secret of spending time with God. He made sure that even though he was busy, his spiritual roots drew upon the resources God has provided. 'Though I am always in haste,' he said, 'I am never in a hurry.' We need to take a leaf out of the great man's book for, if we are honest, too many of us are in a hurry to take time to nurture our souls.

Gracious God, I see that only those whose roots reach down deep into You can stand up under the pressures of life. May all my thoughts be rooted in Your thoughts, and may my will be rooted in Your will. In Jesus' name. Amen.

Where life is found

FOR READING & MEDITATION – COLOSSIANS 3:1–17

'For you died, and your life is now hidden with Christ in God.' (v3)

As we said at the start of our meditations, if we are not careful we can become shallow-rooted and draw our sustenance from things that are superficial; our roots will not go down deep into God. When our spiritual roots go down deep, life's circumstances will not have such a great effect upon us. Rather, we will depend upon God for our joy, productivity and fulfilment. Our fruitfulness is determined by the type of roots we put down. Those with 'surface' roots live by drawing on what they can immediately respond to with their five natural senses. Jeremiah

FURTHER STUDY

Hab. 3:17–18;
Col. 1:3–6, 9–14

1. Why could the prophet praise in bad circumstances?

2. What did Paul pray for the Colossians?

calls this 'trusting in man' (Jer. 17:5). In the lives of such people, what fruitfulness and spiritual vitality there is rises and falls according to circumstances, just as a vine which has roots close to the surface of the soil flourishes or fails according to what happens above ground – rain or drought.

It's sad when a Christian, whose life, as the apostle Paul tells us today, is 'hidden with Christ in God', depends for their wellbeing on the superficial things of life – things such as the state of the stock market, the success of their political party or the school their children attend, their employer's favour or the mood of their spouse. There is nothing wrong with being concerned, or even influenced to some degree, by these things, but they are not where true life is found. Our life is found in God.

Welling up within every Christian is a spring of water that is not dependent on life's circumstances but on a relationship with God. This spring of water flows constantly, regardless of drought. Christians whose roots go down deep have found 'a river whose streams make glad the city of God' (Psa. 46:4).

Gracious and loving Father, You have shown me where true life is found – in Jesus. Although I need to some extent to depend on others, may I recognise that Jesus is the one on whom I can depend most fully. In His name I pray. Amen.

CWR Ministry Events

Please pray for the team

DATE	EVENT	PLACE	PRESENTER(S)
4–6 Sep	Inspiring Women Autumn Weekend: Journeying with God through Transitional Times	Waverley Abbey House	Beverley Shepherd and the Inspiring Women team
29 Sep	Great Chapters of the Bible: The Counter Cultural Wisdom of God that Changes the World	WAH	Philip Greenslade
21 Oct	Inspiring Women Autumn Day: What the Bible Says About Women	WAH	Elizabeth Hodkinson
20–22 Oct	Bible Discovery: With Jesus in the Upper Room – Reflections on John 13–17	WAH	Philip Greenslade

We hope to be 'post-lockdown', running courses and welcoming back our new and returning students to Waverley Abbey College after the summer break, following significant adaptions to remote studying earlier in the year. Please pray for 'business as usual', and for staff and students to be blessed as they begin or resume their studies.

We would also appreciate prayer for our ongoing ministry in Singapore and Cambodia, as well as the many regional events that we hope will be back up and running around the UK this year.

For further information and a full list of CWR's courses, seminars and events, call **(+44) 01252 784719** or visit **cwr.org.uk/courses**

You can also download our free Prayer Track, which includes daily prayers, from **cwr.org.uk/prayertrack**

The mind is the key

FOR READING & MEDITATION – ROMANS 12:1–8

'Do not conform to the pattern of this world, but be transformed by the renewing of your mind.' (v2)

Interviewers have often asked, 'What is the secret of living an effective Christian life?' Well, of course, there are many possible answers, but if they were all condensed to an irreducible minimum I would say this: having spiritual roots that go down deep so that we depend less on life's circumstances and more on God Himself. A close relationship with God provides us with an inner tranquillity and joy – qualities without which life can seem an endless struggle.

I once saw an advert in a magazine for a course teaching techniques designed to bring about stress-free living even in difficult situations. As far as I could tell from looking at the details, the techniques the course promised to teach were those of bio-feedback and relaxation. And although relaxation can help us deal with life's tensions, it is powerless to deal with the soul's tensions. Often the inner conflict of the soul are passed on to the body. Relaxation techniques may help a person to function better, but to have a soul that is free of tension without being close to the one who created it, is another matter entirely.

FURTHER STUDY

Mark 4:35–41;
Phil. 4:4–8

1. Why were the disciples afraid?

2. What precedes the peace of God?

The Message translates today's text like this: 'Don't become so well-adjusted to your culture that you fit into it without even thinking. Instead, fix your attention on God. You'll be changed from the inside out.' A renewed mind can renew our nature. The mind is the key. The mind determines what shall, or what shall not, be the nature of our nature. But the mind cannot be simply told to be at peace and full of joy unless it is resting in some assurance beyond itself. For the mind to be truly at peace it needs to learn to be aligned with the will of God.

Father, I see that although relaxation techniques can be of some help, that which aligns me to Your purposes is of far greater value. I would be right with You and then I shall be right with myself. Amen.

Putting your full weight down

FOR READING & MEDITATION – PSALM 62:1–12

*'Truly he is my rock and my salvation; he is my fortress,
I shall not be shaken.' (v6)*

We have seen that some people try to gain control of life by mastering techniques, ideas and philosophies rooted in human experience. According to Jeremiah, the one who follows this path 'trusts in man' and 'draws strength from mere flesh' (Jer. 17:5). Only as our roots go down deep into God can we be unshakeably calm and poised. As we learn to rest in the truth that God is in control of things, and that a good and benevolent providence is at work, we will be able to remain steady in the middle of life's uncertainties.

I once read about a man flying in a plane for the first time. When asked how he had enjoyed the flight he said, 'Very much, but I never did put my whole weight down.' There can be no enjoyment of a flight or of the larger journey through life unless you learn to put your whole weight down. And there is nowhere in this world where you can rest your full weight, except on God.

Over the years, I have known many Christians who believed that they were duty-bound to worry about the various issues going on in their lives, and that if they did not, then things would go to pieces. One man even argued that all Christians should be pessimists. If we adopt a pessimistic attitude to life, he claimed, then we will not be disappointed when things go wrong. Expecting the worst to happen, he said, will prevent us getting unduly hurt. This is an unhealthy approach to life. When our full weight is resting in the fact that God is with us, even when our plans fail God will, if we allow Him, use the circumstance for our good. As we grow in confidence in the goodness of God, we are more able to handle the things that life brings our way.

FURTHER STUDY

Psa. 16:8–11;
18:1–3

1. Why would the psalmist not be shaken?

2. How did his faith affect him physically and emotionally?

Lord God, forgive me if I depend on old habits of self-reliance, which invariably let me down. Let me live in total dependence on You, my heavenly Father, in working out Your purposes in my life. In Jesus' name. Amen.

A crucial issue

FOR READING & MEDITATION – PSALM 27:1–14

'I remain confident of this: I will see the goodness of the LORD in the land of the living.' (v13)

The issue being drawn out in these initial days of our meditations is that we never fully experience the steadiness of soul that God wants us to have unless our spiritual roots go down deep into Him. As Jeremiah said in the passage we looked at on our opening day, 'Blessed is the one who trusts in the LORD, whose confidence is in him' (Jer. 17:7). So the very first thing we ask ourselves is: How deep is our trust in God and how great is our confidence in Him? One thing is sure: we will not want to know Him deeper if we have doubts about whether or not He can be trusted. After many years of Christian experience I am convinced that it's hard to find peace and remain untroubled unless we are convinced of the love and goodness of God.

FURTHER STUDY

Psa. 23:1–6; 56:1–4

1. How does God care for us when we are tired and in danger?

2. What did the psalmist do when he was afraid?

Sometimes that love and goodness may be called into question by events such as a tsunami or other natural disasters, like storms, wildfires and earthquakes, or when God denies us the things we ask for because they are not right for us. Any doubt about the love and goodness of God is always set against the fact of the cross. A God who loves us enough to give His Son to die for us, and who arranges for those who trust Him to have an eternal home in heaven, has to be good.

We cannot always answer the arguments of those who use widespread catastrophe to question God's character, but we take God by faith. Like the psalmist in today's text, we believe that when all things are finally revealed, God will be seen to have been just and right in the way He has managed His universe. Here on this earth we may be big enough to ask questions, but we are not big enough to understand the answers.

Gracious God, teach me not to rest in the immediate, but in the ultimate. I know that the last word will be spoken by You. And that last word will clarify everything. Help me, like Jeremiah, to take You by faith. In Jesus' name. Amen.

'If not' faith

FOR READING & MEDITATION – DANIEL 3:13–30

'But even if he does not, we want you to know, Your Majesty, that we will not serve your gods' (v18)

For one more day we shall reflect on the thought that there can be no full experience of peace and rest unless our spiritual roots go down deep into God. We need to learn to rest, not in the immediate, but in the ultimate understanding that God knows best, and that everything He does is motivated by His loving heart.

The faith of the three young men in the passage we have read today has been described as the 'if not' faith. This is because they made it clear that if God did not rescue them they would still refuse to worship the image of gold, even though they knew that as a consequence they would certainly burn to death in the blazing furnace. They did not rest their confidence in God's immediate deliverance, but in His ultimate love. To have the faith that rests in the constant goodness and love of God, no matter what we face or whatever happens, is really challenging. However, we read in the Bible many examples of those who trusted in God's faithfulness.

Many years ago I came across these lines, which I then wrote in my Bible:

> *Nothing that happens can harm me,*
> *Whether I lose or win.*
> *Though life may be changed on the surface,*
> *I do my main living within.*

We may face many difficulties and struggles in life, but God has promised to be an 'ever-present help in trouble' (Psalm 46:1). Even when we don't understand or can't see very far ahead, we too can learn, like these three young men, to trust in His goodness and faithfulness.

FURTHER STUDY

Job 13:13–16; Acts 7:54–60

1. How did Job view death?

2. How did Stephen respond when he was being stoned?

Father, thank You for the promise that You allow only what can be turned to good in my life. May the 'if not' faith sustain me as it sustained the young men I have read about today. In Jesus' name. Amen.

Streams within

FOR READING & MEDITATION – GENESIS 49:22–26

'because of the Almighty, who blesses you with blessings of the skies above, blessings of the deep springs below' (v25)

Once, near my home, a row of beautiful trees was brought down by a storm. Speaking about this, someone knowledgeable about trees told me that the probable reason why the trees could not withstand the storm was that the water table was too high – too near the surface – so the trees had not needed to put their roots down deep to find water. Later, when thinking about this, I looked again at the article I had read about the vines in the Napa Valley, California, and came across this: 'Drought stretches the natural vine's root. As long as there is abundant water on the surface the root feeds there, but drought sends the taproot deep in search of moisture. The more frequent and severe the droughts, the deeper the taproot grows.'

FURTHER STUDY

Ezek. 47:1–12

1. What happened where the river flowed?

2. What was its source?

In a similar way, when the things of this world on which we may have been relying fail us, we are challenged to send our roots down deeper in search of spiritual nourishment. We can either find sustenance in the superficial things of life – those of the world around us – or seek to send our spiritual roots downwards to draw from the abundant waters provided by God, which start to flow when we give our lives to Him.

Is there a spiritual drought in your life at this moment? Many of you reading these lines may feel spiritually jaded because you are drawing from the waters found on the surface of life and there is little moisture left. It is important to remember that no matter what happens in life, you always have a choice: you can attempt to find what you need to sustain you in the things of this world, or seek to send your roots down deeper into God. What will you choose to do today?

Father God, help me understand that when I walk down difficult pathways, Your design is to encourage me to put my roots down deep into Your eternal reality so that in stormy times, I shall be unmoved. In Jesus' name. Amen.

Maturity equals trust

FOR READING & MEDITATION – ROMANS 8:28–39

'And we know that in all things God works for the good of those who love him' (v28)

Today we consider the question: Why is it that some Christians put their roots down deep and others do not? After much thought about this matter, I believe it has to do with trust. Jeremiah, I think, would answer the question in this way: 'Cursed is the one who trusts in man, who draws strength from mere flesh' (Jer. 17:5).

It is far easier to put our confidence in the things we can see or quantify than in those we cannot see. It's all too easy to drift into believing that our security and significance depend on things that are tangible, such as money and possessions, academic qualifications, business success, personal skills, or physical attractiveness. However, please do not misunderstand me; these things are not wrong in themselves, but they cannot provide us with the security and significance that deep down our hearts long for.

So it all comes back to this matter of what we depend upon. 'Maturity', someone said, 'is shown by where we place our dependency.' How true. When things don't go as we expected in our lives, we can respond either negatively or redemptively. Responding by complaining, showing resentment, and an unwillingness to forgive prevents our roots going down deeper into God; instead they remain close to the surface. When, however, we trust God and believe that all things are working according to His eternal purposes, our roots start growing deeper and deeper. Sadly, many Christians never gain this trust. Those who grumble and complain when things do not go the way they wish lose a God-given opportunity to develop their spiritual root system. Their roots are restricted rather than extended.

FURTHER STUDY

Psa. 20:1–9; Isa. 31:1–3

1. Where, according to the psalmist, did people put their trust?

2. What are modern-day chariots in which people trust?

Father God, forgive me if I respond to life's difficulties with resentment. May my spiritual roots draw not from the immediate but from the ultimate. Please help me to trust in Your unfailing Word. In Jesus' name. Amen.

What we need to hear

FOR READING & MEDITATION – JAMES 1:1–18

'Consider it pure joy, my brothers and sisters, whenever you face trials of many kinds' (v2)

We are thinking about why some Christians' roots reach down deep and others' do not. We suggested it has to do with trust. Those people who respond to life's trials with confidence that God can eventually turn whatever we face to good, find that as a result their roots go down deeper into God. Thanksgiving, worship and praise during a time of trial has a powerful effect on our spiritual roots and causes them to strengthen.

I knew two Christian women who went through the painful experience of desertion by their husbands. One developed great bitterness towards God for allowing this to happen. Her roots went to the surface for sustenance, and she sought relief in the arts, alcohol and excessive comfort eating. Sadly, life for her became like Jeremiah's unfruitful 'bush in the wasteland' and she was unable to see God's 'prosperity when it comes' (Jer. 17:6). The other abandoned wife, though deeply hurt, began to focus on God, not her distressing circumstances, actively seeking His presence and direction. This resulted in a ministry that has encouraged thousands of other women and drawn them into a closer walk with God.

FURTHER STUDY

Acts 16:19–34;
Heb. 12:15

1. How did Paul and Silas respond to trials and what was the result?

2. What may happen if we do not focus on God?

Unless there is an ultimate trust in the goodness of God in our hearts, we are most likely to turn to that which is temporary for spiritual sustenance when we encounter troubles. When these trials come, do what James suggests: 'consider it pure joy'. George Muller (1805–98), a man of great faith who founded the Bristol orphanages and saw many answers to prayer, said, 'The only way to learn great faith is to endure great trials.' That may be something we don't *want* to hear, but it's what we *need* to hear.

Lord God, I may not always see Your purpose in troubles and trials, but teach me to extend my spiritual roots so that I draw, not from the surface of life, but from the depths that are to be found in You. Amen.

'The great lesson in life'

FOR READING & MEDITATION – PSALM 1:1–6

'But whose delight is in the law of the LORD, and who meditates on his law day and night.' (v2)

Over the past few days we have been reflecting that one of the ways we can deepen our spiritual roots is by putting our whole trust in God in response to the trials and troubles that come to us. There are, however, at least three more things we ourselves can do to encourage the growth of our spiritual roots, and it is these three things that will occupy our attention for the rest of this issue.

The first of those three things is this: spending time with God through reading His Word, the Bible. Christian history bears testimony to the truth that the most influential and mature Christians have been those who knew how to send their roots deep down by meditating on God's Word. Bishop Paul Kern, an American of the Methodist tradition who was known to spend much time studying the Bible, said: 'I read my Bible because (a) within its pages I find power for the ordering of my inner life, (b) it assures me that mankind is supremely dear to God, (c) it tells me whither I am bound and why, (d) in its pages are found the secrets by which mankind walks the pathways of light and hope, (e) it teaches me, in the words of Emerson, that the great lesson of life is to believe what the years and centuries say against the hours.'

Let us consider that last statement, attributed to Ralph Waldo Emerson: 'believe what the years and centuries say against the hours'. What do the hours say? They tell us that things are very uncertain. What do the years say? They tell us that a sovereign God is in control and that we belong to a kingdom that is unshakeable. The more time we give to God's Word, the more unshakeable we shall be in times of trouble and confusion.

FURTHER STUDY

Psa. 119:89–96; Heb. 12:25–29

1. What prevented the psalmist perishing in affliction?

2. What cannot be shaken?

Father, may I become a person who believes what the years say against the hours. Studying Your Word will give me that insight. Please help me get to know it better, I pray. In Jesus' name. Amen.

The Bible – God's corrective

FOR READING & MEDITATION – ROMANS 10:14–18

'faith comes from hearing the message, and the message is heard through the word about Christ.' (v17)

Some people I have met over the years have been of the opinion that it's possible to deepen our spiritual roots without spending time reading and understanding the Bible. Sadly, I do not believe this is entirely possible, other than in exceptional circumstances, for example, if a Christian is in prison persecuted for their faith. I believe the Holy Spirit will be at work, bringing the Scriptures they have previously read to their remembrance. Indeed, there are countless believers who can testify that this has happened.

FURTHER STUDY

Josh. 1:1–9;
Isa. 55:8–9

1. Upon what was Joshua to meditate and what was promised as a result?

2. Why do we need God's Word?

Other Christians use their quiet times to meditate and think about God without recourse to the Scriptures. One person who did this told me, 'I can get to God direct without reading the Bible.' As I talked with this man I could see that his concept of God was drawn from his own thoughts and not from the Scriptures. His ideas about God were nothing more than human thoughts, whereas the Bible is God's revelation of Himself. Unless a person's thoughts are constantly aligned with God's thoughts, they will go in all kinds of unhelpful directions or simply revolve around ourselves.

Like the man who built his house upon the sand (Matt. 7:24–27), when life threatens to overwhelm, there is little or no foundation to hold them steady. As a consequence, they are more easily swayed or even worse washed away in the storms of life. They are easily persuaded to chase after the next exciting or latest fad promising a new, improved and better life. If we build our lives on the foundations of God's Word we will quickly be able to see the diversions and roadblocks put before us and be better able to get back on track when life goes in unexpected directions.

Father, help me understand that the unfolding of Your Word gives light and the neglect of Your Word brings darkness. Please help me walk in Your light for then I shall walk with a steady tread. Amen.

'Deeply Rooted'
to weather the storm

For 55 years now, CWR has been able to support and equip Christians all over the world as they walk Every Day with Jesus. By God's faithfulness and generosity, and the support and encouragement of our readers and Partners, the ministry has emerged from seasons of difficulty and hardship in the past and will endeavour to do so again.

In recent months, the world has been shaken on a global scale by the COVID-19 pandemic, and Christians and Christian organisations – CWR included – have not been immune to the effects of it. We want to thank you all for your continued support through this difficult period, despite the personal struggles and losses you have likely faced yourselves. We'd also like to particularly thank our Partners for supporting us with their finances and prayers; our Board of Trustees and Leadership Team, who have sought God's guidance while making some difficult decisions; and the wider staff, for their continued hard work, perseverance and endurance. So many people have kept CWR going, against the odds, in a number of different ways.

Perhaps now more than ever, we need God's help, and yours, to continue doing the work we believe He has called us to do.

If you would like to become a Partner for as little as £15 a month, please email **partners@cwr.org.uk** or, to make a one-off donation, visit **cwr.org.uk/donate**

Thank you.

The Bible: self-authenticating

FOR READING & MEDITATION – PSALM 119:9–16

'I delight in your decrees; I will not neglect your word.' (v16)

FURTHER STUDY

Psa. 119:1–8, 17–24

1. Who are truly blessed?

2. How could the psalmist behold wondrous things?

Let there be no doubt about it: our Christian life will be reduced and constricted if we do not spend time engaging with the Bible. Some Christians are satisfied with such things as listening to worship music or the sacraments of the Church. One woman told me, 'I get all I need from Holy Communion and reciting the liturgies.' Well, there is no doubt that great spiritual benefit comes from these things, but they are not meant to be substitutes for the Scriptures. John Stott said that a fully balanced and mature Christian life is impossible without regularly reading the Scriptures. I agree.

There are many who wonder how intelligent people can believe in a book that was written before the scientific era, and they accuse us of lacking in intellectual integrity. They charge us with being unthinking – of hiding away from reality and preferring darkness to light. How little they know of the Bible. Non-Christians often view the Bible as good literature or a collection of interesting stories, but to a Christian the Bible is self-authenticating. It speaks to us at our greatest depths. This is because deep answers to deep. We discover it to be a revelation because it reveals – it reveals God to us, and also the condition and needs of our hearts and thoroughly equips the servant of God (2 Tim. 3:16–17).

Scripture is an inexhaustible mine. You may think you have exhausted it and then you meditate on it again and discover new veins of rich ore. Perhaps you need to be encouraged into thought by a devotional aid such as this one, but such guides are secondary and not a substitute for first-hand contact with God. If Jesus – the best Man who ever lived – fed upon the Word of God, so can we.

My Father and my God, You have breathed out Your Word and revealed Yourself in it. Help me to saturate my thinking and my motives with Your mind until I cannot tell where my mind ends and Yours begins. Amen.

FOR READING & MEDITATION – REVELATION 10:1–11

'So I went to the angel and asked him to give me the little scroll. He said to me, "Take it and eat it."' (v9)

More than once the Bible uses a strange expression to describe inwardly digesting the truths of Scripture. It speaks of 'eating' the scroll or the book. One of the many visions that John the apostle received when he was 'in the Spirit' one Sunday while on the island of Patmos was of a huge angel holding a small scroll open in his hand (see Rev. 10:9–10). A voice from heaven told the apostle to take the scroll out of the hand of the angel and eat it. He was to inwardly digest the words on the scroll. Eugene Peterson, when commenting on this passage, writes, 'What the voice from heaven was saying was this: get this book into your gut, get its words moving through your bloodstream; chew on the words and swallow them so that they can be turned into muscle and gristle and bone.'

The instruction to 'eat' the book is a way of saying that the words of God are to be assimilated and become part of the tissue of our lives. If Holy Scripture is to be something more than just words on a page that give us information about God, it is to be internalised. John is being challenged to do more than pass on information about God; he is being instructed to assimilate the Word that comes from Him. Then, when he speaks, the Word will express itself in his message and personality in the same way that the food we eat is assimilated into all parts of our body and issues forth in speech and action.

Every word of Scripture is intended to produce something in us – to give us spiritual health and vitality. It has been said that readers become what they read – providing, of course, they absorb what they are reading. It's not enough to read the Bible; it must be inwardly digested.

FURTHER STUDY

1 Cor. 3:1–2;
Heb. 5:11–14;
1 Pet. 2:2

1. How is the Bible compared to food?

2. Why is the Bible compared to food?

Lord, help me to 'eat the book' – to absorb it and assimilate it so that no matter what might overtake me, I know just how to respond. In Jesus' name I pray. Amen.

Eating the Book

FOR READING & MEDITATION – EZEKIEL 2:9–10; 3:1–15

'So I opened my mouth, and he gave me the scroll to eat.' (3:2)

The apostle John, whom we considered yesterday, was not the first Bible character to be instructed to eat a scroll or a book. Ezekiel, as we see from the passage we have read today, was also given a book and commanded to eat it. Jeremiah, too, 'ate' God's revelation (see Jer. 15:16).

Why did Jeremiah, Ezekiel and John 'eat' the words that came from God? All these men lived in a day when the pressure to conform to the culture of the times was tremendous. Their role as prophets was such that they needed a different text to live by – a text that came from the lips of the God whom they served and whom they worshipped. The diet of Holy Scripture given to them, which they internalised, was such that it enabled them to speak in the most powerful sentences of tensile strength and blazing clarity.

FURTHER STUDY

Exod. 13:1–10;
Deut. 6:1–9

1. How were the Israelites to absorb God's Word?

2. How could God's truth be passed to the next generation?

John, Ezekiel and Jeremiah are good models for preachers who have the responsibility of moulding God's people spiritually in times when there is a clash between Scripture and culture. But first they must 'eat' the Bible. Often many of us – preachers included – treat the Bible as a mere appetiser – something to tickle our spiritual taste buds. However, we hold back from enjoying the full meal. Of course, it is helpful to know even a little of the Word, but only those who take the time to pore over its pages and explore the Book fully will become strong spiritually.

How has the Christian Church survived throughout the ages? Because Christians have been formed by the words of God that they have inwardly digested and absorbed into their spiritual system. The Book became part of them – it got into their blood.

Father, give me an appetite for Your Word, not just in times of trouble, but all day, every day, that I would be strong and able to speak Your Words at the right times. All glory and honour be to Your wonderful name. Amen.

Feeding on Scripture

FOR READING & MEDITATION – MATTHEW 4:1–11

'Man shall not live on bread alone, but on every word that comes from the mouth of God.' (v4)

We spend another day reflecting on the thought of 'eating' the Book. There is a rather sad story of a bishop of Alexandria who, centuries ago, believed the instruction to 'eat the book' should be taken literally, and so he ingested whole pages of the sacred manuscripts. It is said that he was taken ill and died after eating a large portion of the book of Lamentations!

Our text for today tells us that we do not live by bread alone but by every word that comes from God's mouth. Frequently Christians discuss whether or not God intended human beings to be vegetarians when the earth was first created. Veganism and vegetarianism are becoming increasingly more popular. What there should be no argument about, though, is the fact that people made in the image of God are designed to be verbivores – word-eating beings. We survive and thrive physically by the intake of food, and we survive and thrive spiritually by the intake of God's Word. Christians are to feed on the Bible. We are not only to study it but to ingest it.

FURTHER STUDY

Deut. 8:1–3;
Psa. 119:97–104

1. What would cause the Israelites to prosper?

2. How did the psalmist benefit from meditating on Scripture?

The purpose of assimilating the Word is not that we might store it in our minds as information but that it might enable us to live the life God intended for us in the beginning. We can take the Word into our lives in such a way that, to quote Eugene Peterson, 'it gets metabolised into acts of love, cups of cold water, missions into all the world, healing and evangelism and justice in Jesus' name'. When we eat the Book it gets into our bloodstream and becomes a part of us. And when the flood of everyday worries or particular griefs and sorrows overtakes you, the Book is there intact – within you.

Heavenly Father, please help me work up a good appetite and join the apostle and others in Scripture in 'eating' the Book. May it be as necessary to me as my daily food. In Jesus' name. Amen.

Working up an appetite

FOR READING & MEDITATION – 2 CORINTHIANS 3:10–17

'Even to this day when Moses is read, a veil covers their hearts.' (v15)

If, as we have been saying, Christians are to feed on the Bible, and not treat it like a random 'search engine' or some other directory, turning to it only when we are in trouble, then how are we to overcome any reluctance we may have to read the Word on a daily, or at least regular, basis? To put it another way: how do we work up an appetite for God's truth contained in the Scriptures? Here are some suggestions.

First, realise that the Bible is no ordinary book. It is a unique volume. Our understanding of the writing found in the Bible, and the attitude in which we approach it, make an enormous difference. If a man or woman believes that the Old Testament is just a fragmentary record of a few Jewish tribes who lived several thousand years ago in the Middle East, and that the New Testament contains the teachings, which are largely legendary, of a man called Jesus, then they will feel no great need to read it. But if a person believes, on the other hand, that the Bible is an inspired record, and that God Himself has supervised its compilation and ensured that it contains all the information we need to live in a close relationship with Him, then he or she will come to the Book in a completely different frame of mind.

FURTHER STUDY

Psa. 119:33–48

1. What should we turn our eyes away from?

2. How can we walk in freedom?

Every time I open the Bible and turn its pages, I do so with hands that are almost trembling. I am staggered by the truth that I am thinking God's thoughts after Him. So developing an appetite for the Bible turns on how we see the Book. If we see it as, in a very real sense, the Word of God, then we will want to spend as much time as possible discovering and uncovering the truths to be found in its pages and absorbing its great and wondrous truths.

Father, I can see that what makes the Bible so irrelevant to one but so enthralling to another depends on how it is viewed. Let there be no doubt in my mind that whenever I open my Bible I am meeting You in Your Word. Amen.

God's only published work

FOR READING & MEDITATION – 1 THESSALONIANS 2:1–15

'when you received the word of God... you accepted it not as a human word, but as... the word of God' (v13)

Today we continue considering how we can develop an appetite for the Bible, and my first suggestion is, when we open its pages, to keep at the forefront of our mind that we are reading a divinely inspired book – God's one and only published work. God has gone into it and that is why we can expect God to speak to us from it.

When I say that the Bible is the inspired Word of God, I do not mean it is inspired in the sense that John Bunyan's *Pilgrim's Progress* may be said to be inspired. Whatever degree of inspiration may attach to other Christian writings, the Bible is quite different.

J.K. Mozley, a Bible commentator, says: 'In the Christian view of the Bible, it is finally true that it is the Word of God just as it is finally true about Christ that He is the Word of God, and it is almost as difficult in the matter of the inspiration of the Bible as in that of the incarnation of our Lord to draw a true differential between the divine and the human.' The mystery of the incarnation, when God became fully human while remaining fully divine, is truly wonderful. The mystery of the inspiration of Scripture, though different, is also truly wonderful. Although God made use of human writers, He did not surrender His divine authorship or permit the Book to become the word of man rather than the Word of God.

I do not worship the Bible – I worship God – but whenever I take it in my hands my attitude is one of reverence and respect. Had this book not been divinely written, humanity would have been left spiritually bereft. The more we focus on this fact, the more our spiritual appetite will increase.

FURTHER STUDY

Psa. 19:7–11; 119:65–72

1. What makes the Bible uniquely precious?

2. How did the psalmist refer to God's Word, and what did it do?

Gracious and loving Father, may I never approach my Bible with a take-it-for-granted attitude. Clothe my mind with the conviction that it is the very Word of God. In Jesus' name. Amen.

'He did it all'

FOR READING & MEDITATION – 2 PETER 1:12–21

'prophets, though human, spoke from God as they were carried along by the Holy Spirit.' (v21)

Before leaving this issue of the inspiration of the Bible, it might be helpful to consider an illustration used by a preacher called H.O. Mackey – an illustration which brings out the truth we have been considering over the past few days most admirably.

One day in his pulpit, he posed this question: 'Who built St Paul's Cathedral?' Then, replying to his own question, he said: 'It was so many masons, carpenters, iron workers, carvers, painters. But then there was Christopher Wren. He was not a mason, nor an iron worker. He never laid a single stone, drove a nail or forged a railing. What did he do? He did it all. He planned the splendid edifice, inspired with his thought and purpose all their toil and wrought through every worker. They were his "hands" and people today flock in their thousands from all over the world to see Sir Christopher Wren's masterpiece.' When we ask the question, 'Who wrote the Bible?' we have to say that it was people such as Moses, Isaiah, Jeremiah, Peter, John and Paul. They were the human writers, but it is still God's Book. The Holy Spirit used them, with all their individual style and experience, as instruments of His inspirational purpose.

FURTHER STUDY

Acts 1:16;
28:25;
2 Tim. 3:14–17

1. What did David and Isaiah have in common?

2. What is the source of all Scripture, and what is the Bible useful for?

Scripture records three occasions when God wrote with His own hand: at Sinai (Deut. 5:22; 10:2), on the wall of Belshazzar's palace in Babylon (Dan. 5:24), and on the ground in the Temple court in Jerusalem (John 8:6). But it nowhere claims that God wrote the Bible. He is, however, its Author. William C. Proctor has packed this truth into a neat epigram. 'In the Bible', he says, 'we have God's authorship and man's penmanship.' What a book!

Father, what a book! Help me to give myself to reading it with greater abandon. As I come to its pages may my prayer always be, 'Speak, Lord, Your servant is listening.' In Jesus' name. Amen.

How knowledge of God is born

MON
21 SEP

FOR READING & MEDITATION – HEBREWS 4:12–16

'For the word of God is living and active... it judges the thoughts and attitudes of the heart.' (v12)

Continuing our consideration of how we can develop an appetite for Scripture, we turn our attention now to the matter of willing obedience. If we do not engage the Scriptures in an attitude of willing obedience then we will probably quickly lose our desire to spend time reading God's Word.

When Mary was told by the angel Gabriel that she was to conceive and give birth to Jesus, she responded with these words: 'Let it be to me according to your word' (Luke 1:38, NKJV). That's the kind of response that ensures a deeper knowledge of God and the maintenance of a healthy spiritual appetite. John Calvin, the Reformer, said, 'All right knowledge of God is born of obedience.' We are called to be 'doers of the word' (James 1:22, NKJV) – to follow God's message and actively carry out His instructions to us. If there is any resistance in us to do that, it will dampen our desire to know Him better and take the edge off our spiritual appetite.

During my many years as a minister and counsellor, I have often come to find that when a person has lost their eagerness to read the Bible, the main cause has been an issue they thought God might challenge them about. The loss of spiritual appetite was not a symptom of boredom or spiritual lethargy, but was a defensive device making it easier for them to hold on to something that deep down they did not really want to give up. A favourite prayer, taken from the Psalms, which people pray before they read their Bible is, 'Open my eyes that I may see wonderful things in your law' (Psa. 119:18). But what if it is not a 'wonderful' thing we need to be shown, but a challenging thing?

FURTHER STUDY

Psa. 119:57–64;
Matt. 7:24–27

1. What was the psalmist's attitude to God's law?

2. Contrast those who obey and disobey God's law.

Father, I know Your Word is a sharp sword that opens up every part of my life. Help me not to be afraid of what it reveals to me about the condition of my heart, for what is revealed can then be restored. Amen.

Participants

FOR READING & MEDITATION – ISAIAH 42:18–25

'Hear, you deaf; look, you blind, and see!' (v18)

Yesterday we said that if we do not have an attitude of willing obedience, then we should not be surprised if our appetite for reading the Bible is diminished. This is connected with the working of our defence mechanisms, for our instinct is to withdraw from anything that unsettles us.

Another issue we started to consider is that when we open the Bible we may be challenged by it. John Stott puts it like this: Christians who pray, 'Please, Lord, I want to see some "wonderful" thing in your word, may hear the Lord reply, What makes you think I have only "wonderful things" to show you? As a matter of fact I have some rather "disturbing things" to show you today. Are you prepared to receive them? Oh no, Lord, please not, we stammer in reply. I come to Scripture only to be comforted. I really do not want to be challenged or disturbed.' John Stott went on to say: 'When we come to the Bible with our own agendas formed unilaterally, our expectations pre-set, our minds made up, laying down in advance what we want God to say to us, then instead of hearing the thunderclap of his voice all we want to receive is the soothing echoes of our own prejudice.'

The Bible has been given to us so that we can follow Jesus, and if we are not ready to become participants, then we may not fully understand what it is showing us. Instead, we will become bored with it and will settle, as many Christians do, for using the Bible merely as a directory – dipping into it only when we need help in an emergency. Eugene Peterson says: 'The Bible cannot be understood by watching from the stands – or even from expensive box seats. We are in on it.'

FURTHER STUDY

2 Sam. 11:26–12:10;
2 Chron. 18:3–7

1. How did God speak to David through Nathan?
2. Why did Ahab try to avoid the prophet of the Lord?

Father, I see that the more I am willing to obey, the more Your revelation will flow from the Bible into my heart. Help me become a willing follower – a true participant in Your will and purposes. In Jesus' name. Amen.

Training counsellors all over the world

Steve Bradley (CWR Asia Director) brings this update on how work is progressing for CWR Asia.

We believe that God has been calling us to take our counselling training, particularly the Introduction to Christian Care and Counselling (ICCC) course, to Perth in Western Australia. In November 2019, we received welcome approval to use our Asian funding to train some tutors from Australia, New Zealand and Singapore to deliver the ICCC in their localities, and we were also hugely blessed by the generosity of some key supporters, who facilitated many of the practicalities needed for this to happen.

'A brilliant course led by fantastic instructors. I now have some excellent skills for life.'

ICCC – Perth 2020

Through an alumnus of Waverley Abbey College, we made contact with Breathe Counselling, and their team made all the arrangements to make the course such a success, and will hopefully remain key members of the team in Australia going forwards. Tutors flew from the UK to conduct the seminar with 20 students. I travelled from New Zealand to oversee this initial training, accompanied by three potential NZ trainers. Ron Kallmier also flew from Sydney as a mentor for the six Australasians and three Singaporeans.

We had planned to teach the ICCC in Singapore the following week, but with the rapid spreading of the coronavirus, the tutors wisely returned to the UK. The ICCC rollout in Australasia/Asia is now on hold until 2021, for which we greatly value your prayers.

'My experience has been awesome. I've learned a lot and gained some great skills to help people change their lives.'

An odd thing happened

FOR READING & MEDITATION – PSALM 119:97–104

'I have more understanding than the elders, for I obey your precepts.' (v100)

We ended yesterday by quoting Eugene Peterson: 'The Bible cannot be understood by watching from the stands – or even from expensive box seats. We are in on it.' He also tells a story about his love of running. At one time he was so keen on running that he subscribed to three magazines on the subject. But then an injury put him out of action for a while. And he found that an odd thing happened: when he was forced to stop running, he stopped reading the magazines about running. However, as soon as his injury had healed and he started running again, he began to read again. He concluded that he was reading about running not just for information but also for companionship, validation and confirmation. He read in order to deepen the experience he so much enjoyed.

FURTHER STUDY

Psa. 119: 105–120

1. Why could the psalmist avoid the snares of the wicked?

2. How does God respond to those who stray from His decrees?

The parallel with reading Scripture is close, if not exact. If we are not participating in the purposes of God for our lives, and following His instructions and guidance, then we are probably not going to be vitally interested in reading the Bible and discovering them – at least, not for long. Putting into action what God asks of us in the Bible will make us open to what He wishes to say to us – sometimes even more so than through the study of a Bible commentary or handbook. Please don't interpret this comment as a criticism of material written to help us understand the Bible. There is a sense in which studying the Bible is as important as obeying it, for if you don't understand it correctly then your 'obedience' may turn out to be disobedience. When we obey, revelation is given to us and the Book is open; when we are disinclined to obey then the Book is closed to us.

Father, if my appetite for the Bible is diminishing, please help me discover exactly why it is so. If I do not feed on Your Word then I will feed on something else. May I make Your Word my daily bread. In Jesus' name. Amen.

The plans for the future

FOR READING & MEDITATION – 1 CORINTHIANS 2:6–16

'No eye has seen... the things God has prepared for those who love him' (vv9–10)

At present we are looking at different ways in which we can develop a greater appetite for Scripture. Another thing we can do is to think about how vast is the biblical world of revelation in comparison to the secular world in which we live.

There is much talk in some circles of making the Bible 'relevant to the world', as if the world is what really counts and the Bible has somehow to fit in with it. When we read the Scriptures we are introduced to a great wealth of information that, by contrast, makes the material world look small and uninformed. The current culture seeks to figure out the answers to human difficulties through three main avenues: logic, experience, and intuition. The Bible, however, opens up to us another source of knowledge – divine revelation.

The apostle Paul, in today's reading, reminds us that an eternal plan is being worked out, of which the world at large is generally unaware. I once travelled by plane from Brussels to London. Also on the flight were about a hundred members of the armed forces, one of whom was seated next to me. I learned that they had been to a conference about 'The World and its Future'. Apparently no members of the press had been allowed to attend the sessions as the discussions were of the greatest secrecy. Though I did not say this to the person who had told me about the conference, I wondered what those who had attended it might think if I were to stand up and tell them that in my briefcase I had the definitive plans for the future of the world! The Bible gives us not only a view of the past but also a view of the future. It provides us with the best world-view it is possible to obtain.

FURTHER STUDY

Eph. 1:3–10; 3:1–11; Col. 1:25–27

1. What was God's mystery, previously kept hidden?

2. How are God's mysteries revealed?

My Father and my God, our newspapers may give us news about the world, but Your Word gives us news of the world to come. The fact that You are holding the future relieves my anxieties and brings comfort to my soul. I am so grateful. Amen.

Can God tell a lie?

FOR READING & MEDITATION – JOHN 17:1–19

'Sanctify them by the truth; your word is truth.' (v17)

How refreshing it is to know that when we open the pages of our Bible – the inspired Word of God – we are exposing ourselves to a book that tells us the truth. What is so startling and discomforting in today's world is the ease with which people 'spin' the truth. Almost daily news media contain reports of prominent people under investigation because they have been accused of being dishonest. Words of a poem spring to mind: 'Truth for ever on the scaffold, lies for ever on the throne.'

An article I read focused on some politicians who purposefully misled the public; it made grim reading. In the interests of fairness it should be said that there are many honest politicians, but there seems to be an increasing tendency to 'spin' the truth and the proliferation of 'fake news' makes it hard at times to discern truth. One writer said: 'In today's climate it is advisable not to take anything at face value; don't be manipulated by clever wordsmiths who encourage you to buy things you don't really need or even want.'

FURTHER STUDY

1 Sam. 15:29;
2 Sam. 7:28;
John 8:31–36

1. How did David regard God's promises?

2. How can we know the truth and what will it do for us?

With that in mind, how wonderful to read these words in the Bible: 'God is not human, that he should lie, not a human being, that he should change his mind. Does he speak and then not act? Does he promise and not fulfil?' (Num. 23:19). Notice again what the verse tells us: God cannot lie. That is more than saying God will not lie. His nature is such that a lie could find no place in it. If God told a lie then the universe would disintegrate because it is held together by Christ, the Son of God, who said of Himself, 'I am the way and the truth and the life' (John 14:6). The Bible tells us the truth. You can count on it.

Father, how reassuring it is to realise that when I open Your Word I know I am discovering truth. You would never lie to me or fail to act for my good. Blessed be Your holy name for ever. Amen.

'A second naivety'

FOR READING & MEDITATION – PSALM 86:1–17

'Teach me your way, LORD, that I may rely on your faithfulness' (v11)

We talked yesterday about living in a world where more and more people seem to lie with impunity. Paul Ricoeur, a Christian author who wrote on the subjects of philosophy and psychology, argues in his book *The Symbolism of Evil* that it is helpful to maintain a mindset that is suspicious of many of the things that we read about in our newspapers and magazines. In fact, he claims that in a secular world it is necessary. 'There are a lot of lies out there', he says. 'Learn to discern the truth and throw out the junk.'

But then, having adopted that stance, he warns that you should not let it take hold of you to such an extent that you eliminate a trusting view of the world – what he calls 'a second naivety'. Look at the world with childlike wonder, he says; be ready to be startled into surprised delight by the profuse abundance of truth and beauty and goodness that is spilling out of the skies at every moment. See how large and splendid and magnificent life is. What this writer is saying is that despite the many lies that are foisted on us, we should not be blinded to the fact that there are many true things in the world also.

However suspicious we may be of matters in the wider world, there need be no suspicion in our minds when we come to the Word of God. This does not mean that we cannot check the accuracy of the translation we are using or seek to understand the context of the passages we are reading. What is essential is that we approach the Bible knowing that the original manuscripts contain God's truth. Believe me, if you do not have this kind of confidence, then your appetite for the Bible will undoubtedly be diminished.

FURTHER STUDY

Matt. 10:16;
11:16–19;
18:1–5;
1 Cor. 13:11;
14:20

1. How can we combine innocence and knowledge?

2. How can we be childlike but not childish?

Lord, how can I ever sufficiently thank You for giving me a book that guides me through life – one that will never mislead or misinform me? My gratitude knows no bounds. Amen.

Four benefits of Bible reading

FOR READING & MEDITATION – ROMANS 10:1–17

'faith comes from hearing the message, and the message is heard through the word about Christ.' (v17)

Today we ask: What are the benefits that come from daily, or at least regular, Bible reading? First, time spent studying the Bible helps the development of our faith. How does our faith grow? Today's text tells us: by hearing the word about Christ. The more we scrutinise the pages of the Bible, the stronger our faith becomes.

Second, reading the Bible helps us to worship God aright. How can we worship God if we do not follow the guidance He has given us in His Word on this matter? If the right way to worship was not revealed to us, our worship could slide into idolatry. We need to learn what kind of worship pleases God, and only the Bible reveals that. For instance, it tells us that we are to worship Him in the Spirit and in truth (John 4:23). Without the Scriptures we would be like the Athenians Paul addressed who worshipped an unknown god (Acts 17:23).

FURTHER STUDY

Rom. 8:8;
1 Thess. 2:4;
Heb. 11:1–6;
13:16;
1 John 3:21–22

1. Who do not please God?
2. What does please God?

A third thing that comes from exploring the Scriptures is the nurturing of hope. Christian hope is a confident expectation regarding the future. This is why Bible-reading Christians are neither despairing pessimists nor naive optimists. Although all that is happening in the world can fill our hearts with dread and despair, we know God has everything in His hands and will one day come again to this earth to right all wrongs and take full control over human affairs.

The fourth benefit that comes from meditating on the Scriptures is that we are able to obey God. How can we obey Him unless we know His will and His instructions for life? Without a knowledge of these, discipleship would be difficult and confusing. Each of these four benefits come from the revelation God has given us in the Scriptures. Read – and enjoy!

Dear Father, let Your Word be hidden in my heart so deeply that it becomes a spring of action determining my conduct and my character. May I be steeped in Your mind, fired by Your passion, and resolute to do Your will. In Jesus' name. Amen.

The least-used force

'Let the morning bring me word of your unfailing love, for I have put my trust in you.' (v8)

Earlier we said there are at least three things we can do to ensure our roots go down deeper into God. The first we have looked at in some depth – spending time by listening to what God has to say to us in the Bible. We move on now to consider another way in which we may get to know Him more fully – through personal prayer. I have often written on the subject of prayer in *Every Day with Jesus*, and I am convinced of two things: first, there is always more to say on the subject, and second, prayer is one of the most talked about matters in Christian circles and the least-practised spiritual discipline.

I once read a book on prayer that argued that the greatest benefit of prayer is the reflex influence, which comes from quiet thought and meditation. In other words, we become calmer and more peaceful in our disposition because of the time we spend in prayer. Well, that may well be true, but it is certainly not the greatest benefit. I see prayer as this: my lesser spirit coming into intimate personal contact with God's Spirit. Through this contact I come to a common understanding with Him, and so adjust my will to His will, and through that adjustment I become more and more like Jesus.

Those who regard prayer as primarily a reflex influence soon give up on it, in my experience. I agree with the Christian psychologist who said, 'It is not possible to project one's spirit continuously to that which is not responsive.' Many times I have knelt in prayer as a broken person, not knowing where to turn, and God has dropped a word or a thought into my heart that has caused me to arise spiritually reinforced, renewed and encouraged. Has that happened to you?

FURTHER STUDY

Psa. 25:1;
42:1–11

1. How do we lift our souls to God?

2. Why could the psalmist experience hope despite being downcast?

My Father and my God, I am so grateful for this open door of prayer. To be able to communicate with You, the Eternal God, is mind blowing. Yet it is a fact. May I take full advantage of this wonderful opportunity. In Christ's name. Amen.

False ideas about prayer

FOR READING & MEDITATION – PSALM 55:1–23

'As for me, I call to God, and the LORD saves me.' (v16)

Yesterday we said that although prayer can create a calmer disposition, it is false to say that this is the greatest benefit. On one occasion, I made the decision to throw out those books on prayer in my library that propagated false views of the subject. One writer went as far as to suggest that prayer is like a lightning conductor that prevents us being struck by the lightning of God's wrath, which might fall on us if we fail to commune with Him.

Many share the view that if they do not pray then something bad will happen to them. Their prayers, therefore, are not really prayers at all but self-protective devices derived from a wrong concept of God. A young girl once said to her Sunday school teacher in awed tones, 'My mother and father are Christians but we don't have prayer or even say grace in our house – and nothing has happened yet!' I can guarantee that one thing had happened – a gradual distancing from God. This happens so gradually that we are scarcely aware of it, and are not alarmed. Prayerlessness more often results in slow decline than sudden calamity. We either pray or become a prey – prey to such things as anxiety, nervousness and concern.

FURTHER STUDY

Psa. 4:1;
Mark 14:32–42

1. How was Christ's will changed?

2. Why might we not pray?

Another false view of prayer I have come across is the notion that through prayer we change the mind of God so that His will coincides with ours. The purpose of prayer is not to bend God's will to our will; it is to bring our will in line with His. When someone in a small boat throws out a boat-hook to grab the shore, does that person pull the shore to the boat or the boat to the shore? Prayer does not pull God to us but us to God. It aligns our will to His, so that He can do things through us that otherwise He could not do.

Father, I know so much about prayer, and yet so little. Deepen both my understanding and practice of it. Save me, too, from all false ideas about prayer, and lead me in the way everlasting. In Jesus' name. Amen.

Wrong expectations

FOR READING & MEDITATION – PSALM 66:1–20

'but God has surely listened and has heard my prayer.' (v19)

Two days ago, I remarked that I have gone to my knees many times in my life, broken and dispirited, not knowing where to turn, and God has dropped a word or a thought into my mind that has caused me to arise spiritually reinforced, renewed and encouraged. Everything within me said that I had met God.

Often people have told me that they never seem to hear God speak to them when they pray. However, as I have talked to these people, frequently I have found that because a thought did not come to them at the time they prayed, and came some time later, they failed to see it as a direct answer to their prayer. In some instances they did not recognise the thought as coming from God, even though when they acted upon it their life was turned in a new direction. I am convinced that thoughts arise in the hearts of countless people that are in reality answers to prayer, but because they are not accompanied by a thunderclap, or do not come at the moment of prayer, they are not recognised as such. Answers to our prayers are not necessarily dramatic. A quiet thought dropped into the mind by God is as deserving of praise as if the heavens opened and God's voice spoke from beyond the clouds.

FURTHER STUDY

Gen. 50:15–21;
1 Sam. 3:1–10

1. How differently did Joseph and his brothers view his troubles?

2. Why did Samuel nearly miss God speaking?

Ethel Roming Fuller's words have always encouraged me:

If radio's slim fingers can pluck a melody
From night – and toss it over a continent or sea;
If the petalled white notes of a violin
Are blown across the mountains or the city's din;
If songs, like crimsoned roses, are culled from thin blue air –
Why should mortals wonder if God hears prayer?

Father, let me not miss Your answers because of my expectations. Drive this truth deeply into my spirit that You may be thinking in me even when I may not think You are thinking in me. Amen.

Prayer makes it possible

FOR READING & MEDITATION – LUKE 6:1–16

*'One of those days Jesus went out to a mountainside to pray,
and spent the night praying to God.' (v12)*

Today's passage recounts how, after Jesus healed a man on the Sabbath day, some of the Pharisees and teachers of the law 'were furious and began to discuss with one another what they might do to Jesus' (v11). It was just after this that He went out to a mountainside to pray, and He spent the whole night communing with God. So was the hostility Jesus encountered a hindrance to Him as He considered who He would choose to be His disciples?

The Pharisees and religious teachers were so angry with Jesus that they discussed how they could deter Him from His mission. They felt they had the final say, but Jesus countered their resistance to Him through prayer. The Pharisees and teachers consulted each other as to what they would do to Jesus, but Jesus consulted His Father as to what He could do through Him. Prayer made it possible for Jesus not to be a victim of His circumstances – but a victor. Jesus met His circumstances, not from below, but above. As you face the day ahead, do not consider what your circumstances will do to you; ask, rather, what you will do with your circumstances through prayer.

FURTHER STUDY

2 Kings 19:9–19, 35–36

1. How did Hezekiah respond to opposition?

2. What was the result?

Are there circumstances in your life that are conspiring to crowd in and defeat you? Is the last word with them? No, through prayer and the power that comes from your connection with God, decide what you will do with those circumstances. Prayer turns obstacles into opportunities, disappointments into open doors. We can deepen our spiritual roots when obstacles come by responding in prayer. The last word is never with your circumstances, but with God. Out of a difficult situation, and through prayer, came the choosing of the Twelve.

Father, help me to look at all the obstacles that litter my path in a new light. May I not be daunted by circumstances but climb over them through prayer. In Jesus' name. Amen.

Plug in

'pray continually' (v17)

Yesterday we saw how circumstances do not dictate what happens in our day, but how prayer can. Our circumstances may sometimes remain unchanged after we have prayed, but prayer enables us to be strong in those circumstances.

Herbert Spencer, a scientist, said this: 'Whatever amount of power an organism expends in any shape is correlative [or equivalent] to a power taken into it from without.' Similarly, our spiritual lives are determined by the power we take into them through prayer. As I have travelled the world and talked to Christians from all walks of life and all denominations, I have found that the greatest cause of spiritual apathy is the lack of prayer. Many have confessed to me, 'Prayer is the thing above everything else that I want to master, but so often this is the place where I fail.' You can be sure that the devil is bent on hindering everyone's prayer life. The first thing a tiger does when it attacks an animal is to go for its throat in an attempt to cut off its air supply. Satan attempts to do the same with a Christian. By cutting off the oxygen of the Spirit that comes into the soul through prayer, he renders a person powerless.

Most of the casualties in the spiritual life have been brought down by a reduced prayer life. Prayer is pivotal. I am better or worse as I pray more or less. Dr E. Stanley Jones said: 'When I pray I'm like an electric bulb put into the socket, full of light and power. When I don't pray I'm like that same bulb pulled out of the socket – no light, no power.' In prayer our weakness is linked to God's omnipotence, our ignorance is linked to infinite wisdom, our finite self to the one who is infinite.

FURTHER STUDY

Exod. 17:8–13;
Luke 18:1–8

1. What happened when Moses lowered his hands?

2. Why is persistence in prayer important?

Gracious Father, how grateful I am that even when every other way is closed, the way of prayer is always open. Thank You, too, that I am not left alone to flounder in my weakness. My weakness is transformed by Your strength. Amen.

'O God, wake us up to Jesus'

FOR READING & MEDITATION – MARK 1:35–39

'Very early in the morning... Jesus got up... and went off to a solitary place, where he prayed.' (v35)

N o one has ever understood the importance of prayer better than Jesus. His roots went deeper into God through prayer than we can possibly imagine. In today's passage we see that while it was still dark Jesus is in a solitary place – praying. Simon Peter and his companions seek Him out because, in their words, 'Everyone is looking for you!' (v37). In response Jesus says, 'Let us go... to the nearby villages – so that I can preach there also' (v38). Jesus knew that the effectiveness of His preaching depended on the effectiveness of His praying. The impression of the prayer hour became the expression of the preaching hour. Someone has said, 'The most active persons in the world are those who are first inactive in silence.' There, in the silence, they live for a while in the passive voice so that they may live more effectively in the active voice.

FURTHER STUDY

Psa. 5:1–3;
Lam. 3:22–26;
Luke 4:42

1. Why is it good to pray in the morning?

2. Why did Jesus often withdraw from activity?

Alexis Carrel, a Christian writer, says, 'Prayer is the most powerful form of energy one can generate.' Prayer produces spiritual strength within us and enables us to rise above the irritations of the day and focus on moving from task to task with composure and confidence. The prayerful are sure of their directions; the prayerless are frequently hurried, flurried and worried.

A student in a theological seminary tells of the profound effect the principal's prayer had on him and the other students when one day he prayed a single-sentence prayer: 'O God, wake us up to Jesus.' Prayer does indeed wake us up to Jesus. It gives us His awareness and His energy – and shows us that we have access to the same strength and confidence that filled and guided His life.

Dear Lord, wake me up to Jesus! Give me His passion for prayer. If prayer is the most powerful form of energy that can be generated then help me experience more of it. In Jesus' name. Amen.

Cause and effect

FOR READING & MEDITATION – LUKE 5:12–26

'But Jesus often withdrew to lonely places and prayed.' (v16)

We continue looking at the prayer life of Jesus. Today's reading tells us that as the news of Jesus' miracles spread, He often withdrew from the crowds – to pray. Far too many follow after the crowds – and don't pray. Perhaps that's why they fail to draw the crowds, for they have little to give. Preachers are often too conscious of crowds and not sufficiently conscious of prayer.

The reason why the crowds followed Jesus was that they knew He had something special to give. Verse 17 says, 'And the power of the Lord was with Jesus to heal those who were ill.' These two things were cause and effect: 'Jesus often withdrew to lonely places and prayed', and, 'The power of the Lord was with Jesus.' If Jesus had stayed in public places and not prayed, then that too would have been cause and effect. He would have been unable to minister to the people because He had not taken time to be with His heavenly Father in prayer.

FURTHER STUDY

Mark 9:14–29

1. What would overcome spiritual opposition?

2. How did the father express genuine faith and honest doubt?

If Jesus needed to spend a great deal of time in prayer, then how much more do we? Like an old-style watch which requires winding every day, prayer rewinds the springs of life. A prayer room in a Bible college has these words on the door: 'In order to avoid getting lost, use this room as often as you can.' It is so easy to get lost in this world, and we need to come to the prayer time to pour out our thanks to God, to re-orientate ourselves to the spiritual world and to get directions for the day. 'Prayer', says one writer, 'is like the homing pigeon who once let loose circles around for a while to gain a homeward direction. From prayer we go with the homeward direction in our heart. The wings no longer hesitate for the heart is sure.'

Father, day by day the conviction is deepening within me that my prayer life needs a spiritual makeover. If it is difficult to find more time to pray then help me make time. In Jesus' name. Amen.

God's Plan for Your Wellbeing

Brand-new church resource from Dave Smith

The Oxford English Dictionary defines wellbeing as 'the state of being comfortable, healthy and happy'. Others talk of a sense of meaning, purpose, good mental health, satisfaction, or simply feeling well. However, statistics would imply – especially given recent world events – that many people do not 'feel well', reporting stress, being under immense pressure, and feeling overwhelmed. Key ways to improving our wellbeing require us to be aware of how we are doing in various areas of our lives, and seeing how we might take positive steps forward.

The Hebrew word *shalom* perfectly expresses God's passion and plan for our wellbeing. Wellbeing was God's idea and He has the best plan for us. In his brand-new resource for churches and individuals, church leader Dave Smith encourages us to think of our lives as having six different but interrelated 'tanks', almost as if we have dials on our life dashboards. He identifies these as Physical, Emotional, Spiritual, Relational, Vocational and Financial. Each are vital and all are connected; and as such, an increase or decrease in any one of these areas can impact one or all of the others. To help illustrate all of these aspects of our wellbeing, Dave touches on the story of Elijah.

So wherever you may feel you are at – whether stressed, overwhelmed, or simply seeking greater wellbeing in any area of your life – the Bible provides a wealth of insight on wellbeing, and how we can find health, wholeness and harmony with God, ourselves and others.

50 DAY DEVOTIONAL

God's Plan
for Your
Wellbeing

DAVE SMITH

Provisional cover

God's Plan for Your Wellbeing brilliantly
highlights the overview of the Bible when it
comes to wellbeing, looking at:

· Perfect Wellbeing (the first human beings made
  in the image of God);
· Lost Wellbeing (humanity turning their backs on
  God);
· Promised Wellbeing (new covenants between
  God and His people);
· Restored Wellbeing (Jesus' birth, death and
  resurrection);
· Increasing Wellbeing (the Holy Spirit's
  invitation);
· Complete Wellbeing (on Jesus' return).

This resource includes a book offering 50 daily
readings with opportunities to reflect and
respond, along with free online resources that
provide group videos, discussions and sermon
outlines, making it ideal for you, your small group
or your whole church. All available from October.

To register, buy the book or find out more,
visit **cwr.org.uk/wellbeing** or use the
order form at the back of these notes.

Steps to a deeper prayer life

FOR READING & MEDITATION – COLOSSIANS 4:1–6

'Devote yourselves to prayer, being watchful and thankful.' (v2)

Earlier, when we were discussing the importance of reading God's Word daily, or at least regularly, we talked about developing an appetite for Scripture, and I suggested a few ways to do that. Now I would like to suggest some helps for those who might not have much of an appetite for daily prayer. These suggestions are 'scaffolding' that can be taken down once the building of prayer has been established.

First, consider carefully why you do not have a strong appetite for prayer. Is it because there are things going on in your life that you are afraid God might ask you to give up if you get too close to Him? Or is it, perhaps, that you do not know what to say when you come to Him in prayer?

FURTHER STUDY

Isa. 56:3–8;
Mark 11:15–17

1. Why could foreigners rejoice?

2. What had become more important than prayer?

Two people in a close relationship never seem to run out of things to say to each other. Equally, if you feel that you may not know the other person very well, to be alone together could feel awkward and a little uncomfortable. Which is it for you? If it's a little uncomfortable, begin as you might with friend, catching up on the small, everyday things; you'll soon discover our heavenly Father is a good listener and is more than happy to be spending time with you. Or you can begin by thanking Him for His amazing saving grace and the work of the cross.

Second, fix in your mind the importance of placing prayer close to the top of your list of spiritual priorities. Enough argument has already been made, I would have thought, to have convinced you of this. Now start to put what we have been talking about into practice. Commit yourself to deepening your life of prayer by organising your day around your prayer time rather than the other way round. Make it the top priority of the day.

Father, I am beginning to see that nothing I do in life is more important than giving time to prayer. If I stumble, then help me fall on my knees in an attitude of devotion and prayer. Amen.

The climate of prayer

FOR READING & MEDITATION – PSALM 65:1–13

'You who answer prayer, to you all people will come.' (v2)

Today we continue thinking about the steps we can take to deepen our spiritual roots through prayer. Third, remind yourself that God is more anxious than you are to establish this means of two-way communication. Someone has said, 'Prayer is not overcoming God's reluctance, but laying hold on His highest willingness.' When it comes to approaching the throne of grace, we are instructed by the writer to the Hebrews to come 'with confidence' or, as some translations put it, 'boldly' (Heb. 4:16). Because there is one on the throne who has worn our flesh and knows exactly how we feel, we need not be hesitant or shy in approaching Him. His barriers are down. All you have to do is to take down your barriers. Prayer allows God's love and mercy and grace to flow in.

FURTHER STUDY

1 John 4:7–19

1. Why can we approach God and pray confidently?

2. Can you pray back to God verses from 1 John 4?

Fourth, prime your spiritual pump by reading from the Scriptures. Let God speak to you through His Word before you speak to Him through your words. This simple formula (if I might call it that) has transformed the prayer lives of millions. I have been sharing it with people on a regular basis over the years of writing *Every Day with Jesus*. George Muller, to whom we referred earlier, saw the miraculous hand of God at work almost on a daily basis. He said that reading the Scriptures before he prayed revolutionised his times of prayer.

Please keep in mind the fact that I am talking here about building a devotional life of prayer. There will be times of emergency when all you need do is to sit or kneel in God's presence and pour out to Him your concern. He understands that. But experience has shown that establishing a devotional time is best done by first letting God speak to you.

Lord Jesus, help me understand that in Your presence I am changed into Your likeness. I would emerge from every prayer time more alive to You and more alive to others. Amen.

Some further steps

FOR READING & MEDITATION – ISAIAH 50:1–11

'The Sovereign LORD... wakens me morning by morning, wakens my ear to listen like one being instructed.' (v4)

We spend another day considering a few remaining steps we can take to develop our prayer life. Fifth, the best time to pray is in the morning – if at all possible. I say 'if at all possible' as some people may find it difficult to fit in a prayer time in the morning, for instance those getting children ready for school. But generally speaking it is best to spend time in prayer at the start of the day, as it is then forward looking.

After His time of prayer in Gethsemane Jesus said, 'Rise! Let us go!' (Matt. 26:46) – go to meet all that lay ahead of Him. Our prayer times can end in the same way: 'Rise! Let us go!' – go to meet anything, anywhere.

FURTHER STUDY

Exod. 33:15–17;
John 14:6–14

1. What did Moses pray for?

2. What was Thomas' prayer and how was it answered?

Sixth, if your mind wanders during your prayer time don't be dismayed. Many people struggle with this problem of having a mind that wanders during prayer. Pray for the matter to which your mind wanders (if it is appropriate). If your mental wandering has given you another matter about which to pray, then you need not worry too much about it.

Seventh, as I said earlier, be alert to the fact that there may be some things you won't want to pray about. Perhaps there is something in your life that you don't want to focus upon. The psalmist said, 'Surely you desire truth in the inner parts' (Psa. 51:6, NIV 1984). If you suspect there is something in your life about which you do not want to pray, then uncover it in God's presence.

Finally, try to pray less for things and more for a deeper relationship with God. This doesn't mean you can't pray for things, but all the great saints of the past tell us that the deeper our roots go down into God, the more concerned we become, not with getting things, but getting closer to Him.

Heavenly Father, search me and see if there is any hidden sin in me – anything about which I do not want to pray. Help me to bring it into the light. For it is only in Your light that I can see light. In Jesus' name. Amen.

First things first

FOR READING & MEDITATION – PSALM 17:1–15

'Hear me, LORD, my plea is just; listen to my cry. Hear my prayer' (v1)

O ver the past few days we have focused on how, in order to develop our spiritual roots, we need to give time to prayer. Yesterday I concluded by saying that the saints of the past made the point that we can tell when our roots are going deeper into God because we find ourselves praying less for things and more to know God. However prayer is not primarily about whether we get this thing or that thing. If I get to know God then things are merely a side issue.

For many Christians, however, things are essential. A little boy said, 'I love my daddy because he gives me pennies every day.' Penny-praying, like penny-loving, belongs to childhood and immaturity. Jesus taught us to seek first the kingdom of God, and then other things will be added to us (Matt. 6:33).

An elderly saint in Kolkata, India, surprised people in a testimony meeting when he said, 'I would like to burn up heaven and put out all the fires of hell so people will not love God for fear of punishment, or for hope of reward, but will love Him just for Himself.' Though we may not be comfortable with the way the point was made, we can nevertheless understand the sentiment behind it.

FURTHER STUDY

Matt. 11:28–30; Phil. 3:7–16

1. What is Christ's invitation?

2. What was Paul's greatest desire?

Another matter we talked about yesterday was starting the day in prayer. It is good, also, to end the day with prayer. As a camel kneels before its master to have him remove the burdens at the end of the day, so kneel each night and let God lift the burdens that you have carried through the day. Try not to go to sleep without turning your thoughts towards God in prayer.

Do you want to be someone whose spiritual roots go down deep? Then remember, your roots can't grow unless you are prepared to pray – and pray regularly.

Father, I know You are placing this emphasis on prayer not to make me feel guilty but to develop my relationship with You. I ask that You will whet my appetite to want to commune with You more. In Jesus' name. Amen.

The two heartbeats of prayer

FOR READING & MEDITATION – MARK 3:13–19

'He appointed twelve that they might be with him and that he might send them out to preach' (v14)

Writers on the subject of prayer say that prayer has many different aspects, but I agree with Dr E. Stanley Jones who claimed that really there are only two aspects: communion and commission. Everything said about prayer is linked to one of these two aspects. They are the two heartbeats of prayer. Just as a heart has two pumps to keep it beating and to prevent death, so it is also with prayer. Today we focus on communion, and tomorrow on commission.

Many years ago, while I was in Malaysia, I watched some people extracting sap from a small plantation of rubber trees. They would place a cup against the wound they had made in the tree and wait until it was filled before moving on to the next tree. Today there are much more sophisticated methods, but as I watched I thought about prayer, because when we pray we press our empty cups up against God and take from Him life, power and redemption. Every day I love to nestle up to our Lord's wounded side, and I find that if for some reason I do not do that then my cup remains empty.

FURTHER STUDY

Matt. 6:5–14

1. What did Jesus teach about prayer?

2. What are the two heartbeats of the Lord's Prayer?

In the passage before us today we read that Jesus appointed twelve disciples in order that, firstly, they might be with Him, and secondly, that He might send them out to preach, and to have authority over demons. Notice the first thing mentioned: that they might be with Him. Once this first thing is in place – being with Him – and is held intact, then everything else follows. If we neglect communion, then commission becomes exceptionally difficult. When I became a Christian at 16, my father wrote these words in my Bible: 'Empty prayer closet, empty heart, empty hands.' These are words I have never forgotten.

Lord Jesus, You who by Your example showed Your followers how to connect with the source of power through prayer, please give us the will to connect with that same source of power and channel it to other lives. Amen.

Continuous guidance

FOR READING & MEDITATION – ACTS 9:1–19

'Now get up and go into the city, and you will be told what you must do.' (v6)

Following on from what we said yesterday, we look now at the second aspect of prayer – commission. In today's reading we see Saul of Tarsus encountering the living Christ. In answer to his question 'Who are you, Lord?' (v5) Jesus replies, 'You will be told what you must do'. That initial encounter with Jesus on the Damascus Road may have only been a few minutes, but even then he was told to do something. It is clear that he continued in communion with God, and his commission was revealed to Ananias and no doubt Saul too (vv11–16) – communion was followed by a commission.

Communion is frequently followed by a sense of commission, for God wants us not only to be involved with Him but also with others. We are saved to serve, and unless we serve somebody we will become self-centred and caught up with our own concerns. Many Christians are content to include in their lives a church service on Sunday and perhaps a house group in the week. But between those two times of Christian fellowship and worship are great gaps when there is little or no communion with God. If we want to know what God intends us to do, then we are to be in communion with Him continually. He wants to be included in everything that concerns us – directing, encouraging, inspiring.

Those who do not have a sense of guidance in their lives are missing something vital. Today's commission may be different from yesterday's, but how will we know if we are not in daily communion with Him? If we are not being guided by God, then something else will be guiding us – perhaps our own desires. To be self-managed is to be self-damaged, for we are not good enough, and don't know enough, to guide our own lives.

FURTHER STUDY

Acts 10:30–33;
11:4–17

1. What happened when Cornelius prayed?

2. What happened when Peter prayed?

Father God, help me be someone who is guided – someone who follows Your directions, not occasionally but continually. May I discern Your touch upon my life and go where You want me to go. In Jesus' name. Amen.

'At home in God'

FOR READING & MEDITATION – JEREMIAH 33:1–11

'Call to me and I will answer you and tell you great and unsearchable things you do not know.' (v3)

O ne of the things I have noticed as I have read about the great prayer warriors of the past is that many of them had mottos that reveal what they believed to be important in their lives. Francis of Assisi had this as his motto: 'More than I can.' He considered that he could do more through prayer than he could do in His own strength, and think things he could not think using his own mind.

Dr E. Stanley Jones, who long-standing readers of *Every Day with Jesus* will know was one of my spiritual mentors, said his motto in life was 'Not able – but enabled.' And my pastor in my youth, David Thomas, declared that his motto was 'Emptied – to be empowered.'

FURTHER STUDY

Exod. 33:7–11;
34:29–35

1. Where did Joshua spend much time?

2. What happened when Moses entered the tent?

I never considered having a motto for my life, but before I wrote this I paused and asked myself this question: What spiritual motto might I adopt for the remaining part of my life? After much consideration I thought of this: 'At home in God.' I chose it because I was never more at home (spiritually speaking) than when in prayer. If there is one thing I have learned in my life, it is to draw heavily upon God in prayer.

In our text for today God, speaking through the words of Jeremiah, says, 'Call to me.' There are many things I haven't yet learned to do, but I can tell you from the bottom of my heart that I have learned to call. Some would say that calling out to God tends to make us passive and too dependent – unable to stand on our own two feet. But that is not the effect of calling. When we call to God it adds a plus to all our thinking, all our loving, all our acting. God extends His character through us, and in doing so extends our character. We lose ourselves, and in the losing, we find ourselves.

Father, I am so thankful that when You give me Your resources I am able to do more than I can do in my own strength. Through prayer my life overflows with capacities that are not my own. Amen.

Designed by God

FOR READING & MEDITATION – COLOSSIANS 1:15–23

'For in him all things were created: things in heaven and on earth, visible and invisible' (v16)

As we have already spent several days considering the matter of prayer, just before writing this page I prayed something like this: 'Lord, what else can I say about prayer? I have written for so many days on this subject, have I now dried up? Is there anything more I can say?' Then came this thought: prayer makes us natural by our very contact with the one who is supernatural. Through prayer and communion with God we are able to fulfil the purposes God has worked into us through creation.

There is a destiny worked into our beings at the time God created us. We don't produce it; we discover it. That destiny is to do everything in the spirit of Jesus Christ. It is my belief that we are made in the very structure of our being to be Christian. A doctor once told me: 'Because the whole creation was brought into being by Jesus Christ, our bodies and souls have the stamp of Christ upon them. Every organ, every cell, every nerve is intended to work His way. If it doesn't, then it doesn't work well. Our blood runs better when Christ is in it.'

I pondered on this for several days and came to see that we are indeed designed by God to be Christian. When we pray, the supernatural works itself out through the natural, and makes the natural more truly natural. We find ourselves working with the grain of the created universe and not against it. Prayer aligns us with God, and therefore we live as we should – we work out God's intention, which is inherent in the very structure of our being. Our destiny is written not only in the texts of Scripture but in the texture of our inner beings. Again I say it: we are designed to be Christian!

FURTHER STUDY

Mark 16:20;
Acts 3:6–8;
4:5–13

1. How did God and Peter work with each other?

2. What did the Sanhedrin note about Peter and John?

Father, I see that the more I pray, the more infinite power is able to work through our finitude, infinite love through my finite love, and an infinite mind through my finite mind. Thank You, Father, for making me more like Jesus. Amen.

A third resource

FOR READING & MEDITATION – JOEL 2:21–32

'I will pour out my Spirit on all people. Your sons and daughters will prophesy' (v28)

At the start of our meditations we said that a Christian whose roots go down deep has three great resources on which they can draw. We have considered the Word of God and prayer; we now look at the third of these resources – the Holy Spirit.

The Times newspaper, when reviewing a book about the Holy Spirit, said: 'There are few doctrines more perplexing to the average person than the doctrine of the Holy Spirit.' But in the Bible the Holy Spirit is seen in terms of power, not puzzlement. One of the best definitions of the Spirit I have come across is this: 'The Holy Spirit is God in action.' That definition, however, should not lead us to think that the Holy Spirit is merely God's influence, as some believe. He is a separate Person in the Trinity, whose role is to impart life and power.

FURTHER STUDY

Acts 2:1–8, 14–21, 41

1. What happened when the Holy Spirit came to stay?

2. How did Peter relate what happened to the Old Testament?

At the very beginning of time, the Spirit transformed chaos into the cosmos (Gen. 1:2). Throughout the Old Testament we see the Spirit coming upon people temporarily to provide them with power for certain tasks. He came upon Bezalel and gave him the skill needed to build the tabernacle, or Tent of Meeting (see Exod. 31:2). He came upon Samson and 'began to move him at times in the camp of Dan' (see Judg. 13:25, AV).

Always, however, His visits were occasional and at special times. What people longed for was for the Spirit not to come occasionally but to remain upon them permanently. This was the great hope of the Old Testament to which the saints and prophets looked forward. They prophesied that the day would arrive when power would come from heaven to earth and remain here. Today, thank God that the Holy Spirit has come to stay!

Father, help me not simply to believe in the Holy Spirit as a doctrine but as a dynamic. I long to experience more of His power. Lead me on, I pray. Amen.

Waverley Abbey College

'*We are all on a journey of discovery when it comes to the matters of the soul, and it is always good to question what we are saying and doing in relation to helping people and their problems.*'
– *Selwyn Hughes, Founder of CWR*

Our programmes equip students with the skills and knowledge to release their God-given potential to operate in roles that help people.

Central to all of our teaching is the Waverley Integrative Framework. Built on 50 years of experience, the model emphasises the importance of genuineness, unconditional acceptance and empathy in relationships.

Counselling

As society begins to realise the extent of its brokenness, we continue to recognise the need to train people to support those who are struggling with everyday life, providing training to equip individuals to become professional counsellors. Whatever their starting point in academic learning, we have a pathway to help all students on their academic journey.

Spiritual Formation

For those wanting to be better equipped to help others on their spiritual journey, this programme provides robust and effective Spiritual Formation training. Students engage with theology, psychology, social sciences, historical studies, counselling, leadership studies and psychotherapy.

For more information about all of our course offerings available, visit **waverleyabbeycollege.ac.uk** or come along to a free Open Day.

A Christlike Spirit

FOR READING & MEDITATION – JOHN 7:28–39

'Up to that time the Spirit had not been given, since Jesus had not yet been glorified.' (v39)

Following on from yesterday, we ask: Why was the Holy Spirit not given in full measure in Old Testament times? Today's reading tells us that it was because 'Jesus had not yet been glorified'. The fullness of the Spirit could not come until the work of salvation had been completed through the crucifixion, resurrection and ascension.

One theologian suggests that another reason why the Holy Spirit could not be given until Jesus came was so that He could fix our understanding of the Spirit. God's people would then know if they were encountering the Holy Spirit or some other spirit. Jesus, he said, 'not only reveals the nature of the Father but also the nature of the Spirit'. In other words, the Spirit is a Christlike Spirit. This is very important, for some have made the Holy Spirit appear strange. Because many excesses have been practised in the name of the Holy Spirit, some Christians are afraid to surrender to Him in case they, too, become unbalanced.

FURTHER STUDY

Rom. 8:9–11;
Phil. 1:19;
1 Pet. 1:10–12

1. How did Paul and Peter refer to the Holy Spirit?

2. What was the Holy Spirit to accomplish?

In certain parts of the world, small groups of Christians have seized upon one verse of Scripture (Mark 16:18) and believe the evidence you are possessed by the Spirit is that you can handle snakes without being bitten. Over the years, I have come across people who have claimed to have been guided by the Holy Spirit to do things that are clearly against the plain teaching of Scripture. The apostle Paul wrote that 'those who live according to the flesh have their minds set on what the flesh desires; but those who live in accordance with the Spirit have their minds set on what the Spirit desires' (Rom. 8:5). Anything that is inconsistent with the nature of Jesus is not from the Holy Spirit.

Lord Jesus, You have purified our understanding of the nature of the Spirit. I see that the Holy Spirit is characterised by the same purity and holiness that is found in You. And I am so grateful. Amen.

'Sanctity and sanity'

FOR READING & MEDITATION – ACTS 16:1–10

*'Paul... travelled throughout... Phrygia and Galatia, having been kept
by the Holy Spirit from preaching... in... Asia.' (v6)*

We continue reflecting on the thought that Jesus not only revealed the nature of the Father but also the nature of the Spirit. The Christian faith is often called a 'religion of the Spirit', but it is a religion of the Spirit that is defined by the content Jesus gave it by His life and teaching.

Yesterday I referred to a theologian who suggested that the Spirit was not given fully until Jesus came because people needed to understand the true nature of divine power before they could have complete access to it. He may well have been right. There was certainly nothing odd about Jesus. As someone said, 'Jesus was not just sanctity – He was also sanity.' He received guidance through prayer, just as you and I do. He never used the resources available to Him through the Holy Spirit for Himself. During His temptation, He refused to turn stones into bread to relieve His physical hunger (Matt. 4:3–4). He was always in control of Himself and was the most balanced character the world has ever seen. And if we are empowered by the Holy Spirit we will be made like Him. Failure to become like Jesus will reveal that we are not directed by the Holy Spirit but by some other spirit. The incarnation of Jesus fixed the nature of the indwelling of the Spirit. We should not expect the Spirit to exercise any power that Jesus would not exercise.

Did you notice how the terms 'Holy Spirit' and 'Spirit of Jesus' are used interchangeably in today's reading? In verse 6 we read, 'kept by the Holy Spirit from preaching', and in verse 7, 'the Spirit of Jesus would not allow them'. To Luke, the writer of Acts, the Holy Spirit and the Spirit of Jesus were one.

FURTHER STUDY

Acts 8:29;
10:19–20;
13:2–4; 20:28

1. What part did the Holy Spirit play in the Early Church?

2. What part does the Holy Spirit play in today's Church?

Lord Jesus Christ, I am not afraid of being made like You; I am more concerned I will not be like You. If I am not like You then I am not really living. When I am like You then I am living life abundantly. Amen.

The mature stage

FOR READING & MEDITATION – JOHN 16:1–16

'But when he, the Spirit of truth, comes, he will guide you into all the truth.' (v13)

Yesterday I mentioned that the Christian faith is often referred to as a 'religion of the Spirit'. One theologian gives this view: the Old Testament era was 'the childhood stage' when God spelt out in simple terms the truth about Himself. The time when Jesus was here on earth was 'the youth stage', when truth was seen to 'have legs' in the perfect Man who walked on earth as the representative of the Father. Then came the age of the Spirit – 'the mature age' – when power moved into our lives and enabled us to do from within what was previously demanded from without. Because the Spirit dwells within all of Jesus' followers, we are no longer compelled, but impelled. In Old Testament days religion was an imposition, a law; in the New Testament era religion became an indwelling.

FURTHER STUDY

Jer. 31:33–34;
Ezek. 36:24–36

1. Why would people not need to be taught to know the Lord?

2. What did the prophets predict about the Holy Spirit?

Another way of looking at these three stages is this: the Old Testament is God *for* us, the time of Christ is God *with* us, and the age of the Spirit is God *in* us. Let's not be satisfied by 'for' or 'with'; we can only be satisfied when the Spirit is within. The Father's love for His people, as displayed in the Old Testament, is the divine intention; the Son's approach, recorded in the Gospels, is the divine invasion; and the Spirit's work in the age following the ascension is the divine indwelling. God dwelt in a holy Temple, then a holy Person, and now He dwells in us to make us holy. Each time, God came closer to humanity, until He came to the ultimate place – within. The law of the Old Testament became the life in the incarnation, which became the liberty given in the era of the Spirit. And that's the era in which you and I live. How wonderful.

Father, this is where I long for You to be – within. I am grateful that You are above me and with me, but the joy of having You within is joy beyond all bounds. Amen.

The Spirit – from first to last

FOR READING & MEDITATION – PSALM 104:24–35

'*When you send your Spirit, they are created, and you renew the face of the ground.*' (v30)

Permit me to spend one more day focusing on the fact that the Christian faith is a 'religion of the Spirit'. Jesus was conceived by the Spirit (Matt. 1:20), the Spirit descended upon Him at His baptism (Luke 3:22), He was led by the Spirit into the desert and came out in the power of the Spirit (Luke 4:1; 4:14). At the beginning of His ministry He announced that the Spirit of the Lord was upon Him (Luke 4:18). He cast out evil spirits by the Spirit of God (Matt. 12:28), and He offered Himself up as a sacrifice through the eternal Spirit (Heb. 9:14).

John the Baptist predicted that Jesus would baptise men and women with the Holy Spirit (John 1:33), and this was fulfilled when the Church was born of the Spirit at Pentecost (Acts 2:4). We are transformed into Christ's likeness by the Spirit (2 Cor. 3:18). Christians form a dwelling for God through the Spirit (Eph. 2:22). We are given power by the Spirit (Eph. 3:16). The fruit of our Christian lives is produced by the Spirit (Gal. 5:22). Our mortal bodies are given life by the Spirit (Rom. 8:11). The law of the Spirit of life delivers us from the law of sin and death (Rom. 8:2). We receive power to witness when the Spirit comes upon us (Acts 1:8). Every Christian is guided by the Spirit; indeed, if we do not have the Spirit we cannot be a Christian (Rom. 8:9).

FURTHER STUDY

Ezek. 37:1–14

1. What did Ezekiel do?

2. What did the Holy Spirit do?

Need we go any further to be convinced that from first to last the Christian faith is a religion of the Spirit? With all this emphasis on the Holy Spirit in Scripture, why is it that so many churches present a Holy Spirit-less form of Christianity? The Holy Spirit in early Christianity was at the centre of the believers' lives. So He can be in our lives today.

Father, come and flood us out with Your divine power, we pray, until once again, as at Pentecost, Your Church overflows. In Jesus' name. Amen.

Three schools of thought

FOR READING & MEDITATION – ACTS 2:42–47

'Everyone was filled with awe at the many wonders and signs performed by the apostles.' (v43)

We spend some time now looking at a question about which Christians can be deeply divided: How does the Spirit operate in the life of a believer? Broadly speaking, there are three schools of thought concerning this. There are those who say that every Christian has all of the Spirit's resources available to them from the time of their initial surrender to Jesus. Our problems arise, they say, when we fail to draw from the Spirit's resources and utilise them in our daily living.

Another school of thought argues that what we receive at the time of our initial surrender to the Saviour is not the Holy Spirit, but 'the spirit of Christ'. They see 'the spirit of Christ' as different from the Holy Spirit, and thus all Christians, they maintain, should seek the blessing of the Holy Spirit after their conversion.

A third school of thought claims that every Christian is indwelt by the Spirit from the time of their initial commitment to Christ, but that there is further work of the Spirit within which we experience according to our willingness to open up to the Spirit's power.

FURTHER STUDY

Matt. 3:1–3,11;
Acts 1:1–8

1. What did John promise?

2. What were the disciples to wait for?

Whatever school of thought you agree with, the question I would put to you now is this: Is the Holy Spirit at work in your life in the way He was in the lives of the believers immediately after Pentecost as shown in Acts 2:42–47? If we are honest, almost every one of us, and I have included myself in this, will admit that compared to the early Christians we seem to lack dynamism and spiritual power. Let's open more of ourselves to Him, and cry from the depths of our heart, 'Holy Spirit, fill my life with Your might and power, and fill it to overflowing.'

Yes, my Father, however much Your Spirit is at work within me, I know I need Him more. Fill me with Your Holy Spirit so that I will be all-glorious within and adequate for anything without. In Jesus' name. Amen.

'To be continued'

FOR READING & MEDITATION – ACTS 4:23–31

'And they were all filled with the Holy Spirit and spoke the word of God boldly.' (v31)

It is my hope that at this stage you will not be so taken up with the doctrine of the Holy Spirit (though sound doctrine is most definitely important) that you will fail to take hold of His power. As I said yesterday, whichever view we might take of how the Holy Spirit operates in the life of a person, it should not hinder us from crying out, 'Holy Spirit, fill my life with Your might and power, and fill it to overflowing.'

A very good minister friend said this to me some years ago: 'I went to my doctor because I was feeling run down, and he told me that I was probably trying to build a £100,000 house with only £50,000 resources.' That diagnosis, I imagine, could be given to many other Christians – perhaps even to you. Many are trying to do things they would not be doing if they were guided by the Spirit, or trying to do them in their own strength rather than His – hence the strain.

FURTHER STUDY

Gen. 26:12–32

1. How did Isaac obtain water?

2. What did Isaac's enemies do?

Somewhere I read that in the early days of the oil boom in Texas, oil was pumped from near the surface until the supply became meagre. Then an oil baron dared to go down 5,000 feet and struck new levels of oil, which brought forth great gushers. Now I understand almost all the oil is tapped at these low levels.

One of the great challenges we face as Christians is to go down to the deeper levels and tap the resources of the Spirit which are available to us. Then we will be artesian and overflowing. The early Christians were like this; the Holy Spirit flowed out from within them. They turned the world upside down (see Acts 17:6, AV). And what they began we can continue. 'To be continued' is not written at the end of the Acts of the Apostles, but it is most certainly implied.

Holy Spirit, again I ask that You teach me how to take hold of Your inexhaustible resources. Please turn my difficulties into encouragements, my impurities into purity, my minuses into pluses. In Jesus' name. Amen.

Running smoothly

FOR READING & MEDITATION – EPHESIANS 3:12–21

'I pray that out of his glorious riches he may strengthen you with power through his Spirit in your inner being' (v16)

Yesterday we spoke about the oil barons of Texas who in the early days pumped oil from near the surface until the supply became meagre. Then someone dared to go down 5,000 feet and struck new levels of oil, which brought forth great gushers. The story is told of Chinese visitors who came to look at the Texas oil wells. As they approached one, they were surprised that it was squeaking. They couldn't understand why a well that pumped oil should squeak so badly. While they stood around wondering, an engineer came along and oiled the machinery that was squeaking. One member of the party commented, 'I thought an oil well would take care of itself without the need for oiling.' They appeared not to understand that the machinery that pumped oil needed oil in order to work efficiently.

FURTHER STUDY

Judg. 15:9–19

1. How did Samson overcome the Philistines?

2. How did he feel afterwards and what did he do?

That story prompted me to ask: How vital is it for the Holy Spirit to put oil into the machinery of a Christian worker's life when he or she is trying to pump oil for others? Unless our own machinery is running smoothly people will not believe we have oil for the needs of others. How can we witness to others if it is obvious that our own lives are somewhat squeaky?

A prominent and discerning layman of the Church of England once said this: 'The present level of Christianity seems to have exhausted itself against the problems of the present day. It will have to be renewed on a deeper level if it is to become functionally adequate.' That deeper level is nothing less than the power evident at Pentecost, which should become our working capital. When we, as Christians, go down to that deeper level and tap the resources which are there for us, then we shall function far more powerfully.

Father, I must ask myself if I have experienced the fullness of the Spirit. I have to confess I know there is so much more. Take me deeper, Lord, until I discover Your endless power in my life. In Jesus' name. Amen.

Precepts – not enough

FOR READING & MEDITATION – MARK 6:45–56

'They begged him to let them touch even the edge of his cloak, and all who touched him were healed.' (v56, NIV 1984)

During my years as a minister of the gospel, one of the things that has saddened me is that many people seem to rely more on their own strength to live out the Christian life than they do on the power of the Holy Spirit. As I have said many times before, the Christian life is not our *responsibility*, but our response to His ability.

Early in my Christian life I went into my prayer time one day asking myself this question: Am I relying on my own abilities rather than on the Holy Spirit's power? Later, towards the end of my prayer time, God seemed to whisper to me, 'Yes, you are depending more on your reserves than on my resources.' That led, as you can imagine, to a time of deep soul-searching, but the result was moments of utter abandonment to the Holy Spirit. By the way, that question might be a good one to ask yourself as you begin your own prayer time today.

Often it is at the point of power that we break down. Many of us live by biblical precepts, but we are devoid of power. Our text highlighted for today tells us that 'all who touched him were healed'. It wasn't enough that power left Jesus; it was also necessary to touch Him in faith. And it is the same when it comes to moving in the power that the Holy Spirit gives; we have to reach out to Him, confess our inability to function effectively in our own strength, and send our roots down deep to draw on the resources that the Holy Spirit gives. I once saw some words on a school blackboard that read, 'I can do little; we can do anything.' That can be said, too, of the Christian life. On our own we can accomplish little; with the help of the Holy Spirit we can do anything.

FURTHER STUDY

Judg. 7:1–9;
Zech. 4:6

1. Why was Gideon's army too large?

2. How does God accomplish things?

Holy Spirit, I long to be indwelt and strengthened by Your divine power. May I go out into the day, not on my own, but conscious that You are with me. In Jesus' name. Amen.

'A perfect Gentleman'

FOR READING & MEDITATION – 1 CORINTHIANS 14:26–40

'The spirits of prophets are subject to the control of prophets.' (v32)

There are many Christians, I have found, who are cautious to have anything to do with the Holy Spirit. They believe in the Holy Spirit but are nervous about opening up to Him because they know He is the source of divine power.

One such Christian said to me, 'I'm afraid to open up to the Holy Spirit because He might make me emotional and cause me to speak in other tongues, or pressure me to give my testimony to everyone I meet.' This reminded me of an old story from Malaysia about a wealthy man who sat in his new Ford car and had his servants push him up and down the street. When asked if there was any power in the car he replied, 'Yes, but I'm afraid to turn it on.'

FURTHER STUDY

Isa. 55:1–6;
Matt. 26:49–54;
Luke 14:16–24;
Rev. 3:20

1. How does God relate to us?

2. Why does He not use force to control us?

How many other Christians, I wonder, are like that? Unbelievable resources are available but they are afraid to step out in trust. Are any of you reading this apprehensive about surrendering to the Holy Spirit because you fear that you might become emotional and unbalanced? Certainly, some people claim to be filled with the Spirit but act in ways that are strange and off-putting. That, however, cannot all be levelled at the Holy Spirit. It's more about people, their responses and reactions, for the Holy Spirit will never push anyone beyond the point of their own control.

Today's text reminds us that the spirits of prophets are subject to the control of the prophets, meaning that God does not ride roughshod over our personalities, although He will take us beyond our personalities and enable us to do more in His strength than we can in our own. 'The Holy Spirit', my old pastor used to say, 'is a perfect Gentleman.' He leads and guides but He will never override.

Father, please take away any fears I may have concerning surrendering to Your Holy Spirit. Your Word says that You give good gifts to Your children. So I surrender. Anoint me afresh with Your Spirit this very hour. In Jesus' name. Amen.

Next Issue

Nov/Dec 2020

More Than Conquerors

We live in extraordinary times, two thousand years after the apostle Paul wrote his letter to the Romans. Yet he, also writing during a season of hardship, was able to celebrate the wonderful truth that nothing can separate us from the love of Christ – and by His great love for us, we are more than conquerors.

Next issue, join us as we explore Paul's exhortations in Romans 8 and what it means to be a 'conqueror'. And slightly later in December, we'll move into a special time of Advent reflection, when we'll marvel afresh at the wonder of Christ's incarnation.

Every Day
with Jesus
NOV/DEC 2020

More Than Conquerors

'If God is for us, who
can be against us?'
Romans 8:31

Living life with Jesus. Every day

CWR

Also available as an
eBook/eSubscription

The vital imperative

FOR READING & MEDITATION – JOHN 14:15–31

'And I will ask the Father, and he will give you another advocate to help you and be with you for ever' (v16)

A week ago we said that the divine intention, which we see in the Old Testament, became the divine invasion through the coming of Jesus into the world, and the divine invasion resulted in the coming of the Holy Spirit to the world – the divine indwelling. It is not enough to have redemptive intention and invasion. Both are outside of us and therefore not fully adequate, for our needs are within us. For the gospel to be complete there is an initiation to a divine indwelling.

A critic of Christianity once wrote: 'The Christian faith is a counsel of perfection, making impossible demands on human nature.' He showed by that statement that he knew little of the Christian message. God does call us to live in a way that is impossible to human nature, but He is there to provide the power and strength to enable us to meet His calling. And the power that He gives us comes to us through the Holy Spirit. In the incarnation, God came and lived among us, but through the indwelling of the Holy Spirit He comes into us – into the very core of our being. And He comes alongside us, as today's text says, as our Advocate, to be with us for ever.

FURTHER STUDY

Acts 19:1–7;
1 Thess. 5:19

1. What was Paul's question to the disciples?

2. What should we beware of?

During a sermon a minister suggested to his congregation that 'the Holy Spirit comes and goes as we need Him'. That cuts at the very root of the doctrine of the divine indwelling. It is Old Testament theology. Thank God we have both the Old and the New Testaments, and the truth taught in the New Testament is that the Spirit comes to abide with us. All He asks is that we make Him welcome. Many Christians say rather proudly, 'I have the Holy Spirit.' But even if He is residing within you, are you giving Him full sway in your life?

Heavenly Father, again I ask that You will help me to welcome You into my life. Help me not attempt to work out things on my own. I long to be strengthened through this divine–human togetherness. In Jesus' name. Amen.

It's all empty inside

FOR READING & MEDITATION – ROMANS 15:1–13

'May the God of hope fill you with all joy and peace... so that you may overflow with hope by the power of the Holy Spirit.' (v13)

Having talked in general terms about putting our roots down deep to draw on the resources of the Spirit, we now consider the steps we take to do that. As I mentioned earlier, I realise readers may have different views concerning the way in which the Spirit works in the life of a believer. I have no desire to change anyone's theological beliefs regarding the Spirit, but I do have a desire to encourage you to draw more deeply from His resources. So what I propose to do over the next few days is to offer some suggestions that will apply to us all, irrespective of the view you may have of how the Holy Spirit operates in your life.

FURTHER STUDY

Rom. 14:17; Eph. 5:15–20

1. What characterises the kingdom of God?

2. What should we be full of?

First, ask yourself: How conscious am I of the Holy Spirit being present in my soul and at work in my life? I am aware that I asked you to consider a similar question the other day, but some may have missed it or not been ready for it.

I once addressed a ministers' conference in South Wales on the subject 'A Christian minister and the Holy Spirit'. After I had finished speaking, a minister stood up, put his hand over his heart, and said, 'It's all empty inside.' Later, I met this man to talk and pray with him, and I asked him what he meant when he declared he was empty inside. His reply was significant. 'I meant,' he said, 'that I have been functioning using my own abilities, such as my preaching ability, my knowledge of the Scriptures, and my understanding of Greek and Hebrew – so much so that the Holy Spirit has been pushed aside. I'm empty in the sense that the strength by which I operate is human rather than divine.' Anyone who functions by relying on human abilities alone will inevitably feel empty inside.

Holy Spirit, thank You that You promise to fill me to overflowing. Fill me up. Help me open up my whole being to Your presence and power. I do so now. In Jesus' name. Amen.

Running half-empty

FOR READING & MEDITATION – REVELATION 3:14–22

'So, because you are lukewarm – neither hot nor cold – I am about to spit you out of my mouth.' (v16)

At present we are considering some practical things we can do to send our roots down deep and draw on the Holy Spirit's resources. The first thing we do, we said, is to examine our hearts and determine to what extent the Spirit's power is at work in our lives. Are you like the minister we talked about yesterday, who put his hand over his heart and declared, 'It's all empty inside'? Some reading these lines might say, 'Well, I'm not exactly empty, but perhaps I'm half-empty.' Let me tell you that being 'half-empty' is very precarious place. In fact, I would go as far as to say it is better to be empty than half-empty.

FURTHER STUDY

Matt. 15:1–9;
Luke 18:9–14

1. Why were the Pharisees criticised despite their religious practices?

2. Why was the tax collector accused by God?

The church in Laodicea, in today's reading, was challenged by Jesus for being 'lukewarm'. Being lukewarm is the same as being half-empty. The metaphor changes but the condition is the same. And what is that condition? It is complacency. I believe complacency is one of the worst states in which we can find ourselves spiritually. And this is the reason why: when you are complacent you compare yourself to other Christians who are spiritually empty and you say to yourself: 'Well, I'm not like them. At least I'm allowing the Spirit to have some say in my life.'

Jesus said to the Laodiceans, 'I wish you were either one or the other – cold or hot.' Similarly, I think He would address those who are half-empty and say, 'I wish you were either empty or full.' Being half-empty can make you complacent. 'Be filled with the Spirit' was Paul's plea to the Ephesian Christians, and the tense of the Greek means to go on being filled by the Spirit (Eph. 5:18). Half-full is not enough. Fullness is what God wants for all of us.

God, Your Word strikes deep into my soul. If I have become complacent in my spiritual life, then shake me out of it I pray. And do so today. In Jesus' name. Amen.

Ask, seek, knock

FOR READING & MEDITATION – LUKE 11:1–13

'how much more will your Father in heaven give the Holy Spirit to those who ask him!' (v13)

Throughout my life, whenever I have attempted to minister to people who wanted to open up their lives more fully to the Holy Spirit, I have tried to help them by inviting them to consider three simple issues – all of which, I believe, are drawn from Scripture.

First, we ask the Father to give us His Holy Spirit. This point is made most clearly in today's text. Many times when Christians have lamented the fact that they lacked the Spirit's power I have said to them, 'Have you asked God to fill you with His Holy Spirit – to fill you to overflowing?' And so often they have realised that they have spent time bemoaning their lack of power instead of asking God to remedy the situation.

FURTHER STUDY

Gen. 32:22–30; John 14:13–14; 16:24

1. What was Jacob's attitude?

2. What was Jesus' promise?

In verse 9 Jesus shows that there are three stages when it comes to petitioning Him: asking, seeking and knocking. Asking sometimes needs to be intensified into seeking, and seeking into knocking. When you knock you are right on the threshold – right on the verge of entering. The wording used depicts a person who longs for the Holy Spirit with such intensity that he or she is totally unable to live without Him. When your intensity causes you to knock, realise that the door is not a barrier but a means of entrance. Our hearts will never be flooded by the Spirit until we come to the realisation that we cannot live without Him.

Many years ago I attended a prayer meeting where those present were asking to be filled with the Spirit. As the time came for the meeting to close, a friend said to me, 'Leave the keys, I'll lock up. I'm not leaving here until I have what I came for.' I decided to stay with him, and within 15 minutes he had received an infilling of the Spirit that transformed his life.

Father, I am not entering this quest lightly. I need to be filled to overflowing with Your Spirit. May I set my face and my life to seek and find. In Jesus' name. Amen.

Surrender or dedication

FOR READING & MEDITATION – ROMANS 8:1–17

*'those who live in accordance with the Spirit have their minds set on
what the Spirit desires.' (v5)*

The point we are making is that when we are seeking to experience the fullness of the Spirit we cannot think that we will receive it automatically. The first thing we do is to ask God for His Spirit. Second, we open ourselves to the Spirit by an act of faith. This involves surrender. Often surrender is regarded as being the same as dedication. It isn't. In dedication you still retain whatever you are dedicating (your talents, abilities, education, and so on) whereas in surrender you let go.

FURTHER STUDY

Luke 21:1–4;
Acts 5:1–11

1. How did the widow show her total surrender to God?

2. What did Ananias and his wife do?

The following illustration may trouble those of you who are literally minded because you may argue that inanimate objects cannot surrender to anything simply because they are inert and lifeless. However, indulge me, if you will. Just as a canvas surrenders itself to a painter, a violin to a musician, a wire to electricity, so, in surrendering to the Holy Spirit we put ourselves at the disposal of the one who is divine. If you ask for the gift of the Spirit Himself then you also surrender yourself. You cannot ask the Spirit for the gift of Himself and not give your own self.

The Holy Spirit is waiting and ready to give Himself to you in all His fullness, but He can only do so as you give yourself to Him in all your fullness. This means holding nothing back, no half-heartedness, no saying to yourself, 'Well, I still have talents and abilities to fall back on.' It doesn't work that way. And what is required is not just an initial surrender. Surrender in marriage is once-and-for-all but yet continuous. Paul could say, 'I have been crucified with Christ' (Gal. 2:20), and yet, 'I face death every day' (1 Cor. 15:31). Appropriating faith reaches out on a daily basis.

Father, I am grateful for everything You have done for me through Your Holy Spirit, but now I reach out for more. In my heart, a cry – in Your heart, supply. May the two come together, now. In Jesus' name. Amen.

'I am Your obedient servant'

FOR READING & MEDITATION – ACTS 5:17–32

*'We are witnesses of these things, and so is the Holy Spirit,
whom God has given to those who obey him.' (v32)*

Now we look at the third of the issues which enable us to experience more of the Holy Spirit: an attitude of continuous obedience. Over the years, I have come across a number of Christians who, when they have heard that someone has had a dynamic encounter with the Spirit, have longed for a similar experience. But their desire has been for a supernatural experience and not to deepen their spiritual roots. So many people are attracted to and more concerned about experiencing something supernatural than getting to know God more fully. That is why we now turn to our text for today, which tells us that God gives the Holy Spirit to those who obey Him.

The word 'obey' found in this verse is in the present tense in the original Greek. This indicates that we are to obey God continually. It is not enough to obey in the sense of opening our life up to an encounter with the Spirit; it means being willing to follow Him and be guided by Him today, tomorrow, and all the days thereafter. You can rest assured that the Holy Spirit will stay in 'residence' as we respond to all He says and instructs. When we take over, He quietly withdraws. He will never take over and control us until we give the reins to Him once more and obediently allow Him to lead and guide and direct.

The difference between the life of faith and the life of the world, it has been said, is this: 'The pagan heart says: know yourself, accept yourself, develop yourself. The Christian heart says: surrender yourself, discipline yourself, obey another Self.' That other Self, of course, is the Spirit of God. We are made to be under His direction, and when we are governed by Him we find life and fulfilment.

FURTHER STUDY

1 Sam. 15:1–3, 9, 17–23;
Acts 5:29

1. Why did Saul claim to have obeyed the Lord?

2. What is better than sacrifice?

Spirit of the living God, I consent – gladly consent – to You directing my life. May I be willing to say every day, 'I am Your obedient servant.' In Jesus' name. Amen.

Roots and fruit

FOR READING & MEDITATION – MATTHEW 3:1–12

'every tree that does not produce good fruit will be cut down and thrown into the fire.' (v10)

We are drawing close now to the end of this issue in which we have thought about the need to deepen our spiritual roots, and just one question remains: Why is all that we have covered over the past weeks important? Is it only that we might experience a stronger sense of peace and joy? No, it is because primarily what our heavenly Father is looking for in our lives is spiritual fruit. And, as we said earlier, the deeper our roots go down, the more fruit will grow up.

You may remember I said at the start that the idea for this issue came after I read about a person who had visited a vineyard in the Napa Valley, California. He was amazed when the manager of the vineyard told him the tap roots of some vines can go down 30 or 40 feet to reach the water table. Some might question the depth of 30 to 40 feet, but that is what the manager claimed, and, of course, he should know. However, vines do not only need a supply of water; they also need careful pruning. Maximum fruitfulness is obtained when a vine has plenty of water and is pruned in the correct way. A viticulturist knows that it is possible to have luxuriant growth but no fruit. The useless non-fruit-bearing growth – the shoots that take life but give no fruit – must be cut away. Today's text warns, 'every tree that does not produce good fruit will be cut down and thrown into the fire.' Life involves not only assimilation but also elimination.

Another thing we have already said but which we must keep in mind is that Christian growth is not automatic; it happens only as we do our part in co-operating with the work of the Spirit within us (Phil. 2:12–13). We do our part; He does His.

FURTHER STUDY

Psa. 92:12–15;
Matt. 21:18–19;
Luke 13:6–9

1. What will happen to the righteous?

2. What is Jesus' attitude to trees?

Gracious and loving heavenly Father, I am so grateful that while I work on deepening my life, You are working on developing it also. You cut, not for the sake of cutting, but to cure, to conserve and contribute. Amen.

The Divine Gardener

FOR READING & MEDITATION – JOHN 15:1–17

'every branch that does bear fruit he prunes so that it will be even more fruitful.' (v2)

In these final days, we are saying that the purpose of our meditations has not been simply to gain a stronger sense of peace and joy. No, what has prompted our studies is the fact that, primarily, what our heavenly Father is looking for in our lives is spiritual fruit. The text we looked at yesterday – Matthew 3:10 – made it clear to us that being fruitful is a serious business. More than anything, God wants to see fruit appearing in our lives. He desires to see it, and He wants others to see it also.

Today's reading tells us the same thing. In the New Living Translation the first two verses of John 15 are translated in this way: 'I am the true grapevine, and my Father is the gardener. He cuts off every branch of mine that doesn't produce fruit, and he prunes the branches that do bear fruit so they will produce even more.' So while we work on deepening our spiritual roots by reading the Word of God, by prayer, and by being more open to the Holy Spirit, our heavenly Father works on us by pruning the branches of our lives. And what for? That we might become more fruitful. Our heavenly Father, the Divine 'Gardener' as the New Living Translation refers to Him (John 15:1), is involved not only in helping us develop our roots but also above ground where the fruit is to be seen. He prunes us into fruitfulness and beauty. The open secateurs might look intimidating, even menacing, but consider in whose hand they are held. Hold steady, for the pruning will result in a greater yield of fruit.

Over the years, I have suggested many prayers to end the day's meditations, but none is more important than this. I invite you to pray it with me now:

FURTHER STUDY

Matt. 21:33–43;
Gal. 5:22–23

1. What does God desire from His servants?

2. What is the fruit God is looking for?

Divine Gardener, may I always be willing for You to show me the difference between the useless and the useful, and allow You to prune me for greater productivity in Your kingdom. For Jesus' sake I ask it. Amen.

A fruitful vine

FOR READING & MEDITATION – 1 JOHN 5:13–21

'This is the confidence we have in approaching God: that if we ask anything according to his will, he hears us.' (v14)

Today we end our meditations on the theme of being Deeply Rooted. This issue has been written out of a desire to help Christians draw from God's resources as opposed to self-reliant strategies. Far too many believers rely solely on what they get from church services, from sermons, and from the singing of hymns and worship songs. Although these things are important and helpful, they are not intended, as I have repeatedly emphasised, to be a substitute for reading the Word daily (or at least regularly), for prayer and being open to the Holy Spirit.

FURTHER STUDY

Psa. 1:1–6;
Isa. 37:30–31

1. How can we feed ourselves?

2. What happens below and what happens above?

There are certain things God expects us to do in order to deepen our spiritual roots, and if we fail to do them, then He cannot do them for us. Ignoring these disciplines will cause us to become, as Jeremiah so graphically put it, 'like a bush in the wastelands' (Jer. 17:6). Unless there is a deep yearning in us for the things of God we will turn to that which is temporal to fill our lives – the things of the world around us.

So settle the matter once and for all by telling God that you want Him to help you send your spiritual roots down deep into Him. Martin Luther, the Reformer, is reported to have said, 'Ask God to work faith in you, or you will remain forever without faith, no matter what you wish, say, or do.' Faith, or obedient trust, is the root through which spiritual nourishment is drawn into our lives. This is then transformed into rich and abundant fruit. So have faith in God and surrender your whole life to Him. He longs for you to prosper spiritually, but you must long for this too and be prepared to do what He requires you to do. When you do, then, like Joseph, you will be a 'fruitful vine' (Gen. 49:22).

Father, thank You for the challenges You so gently and lovingly bring to my life. For where there is no challenge there can be no change. May my life continually be a response to all You are revealing to me. In Jesus' name. Amen.

Easy Ways To Order

Phone in your credit card order: **01252 784700** (Mon–Fri, 9.30am – 4.30pm)

. Visit our online store at **cwr.org.uk/store**

. Send this form together with your payment to: **CWR, Waverley Abbey House, Waverley Lane, Farnham, Surrey GU9 8EP**

. Visit a Christian bookshop

a list of our National Distributors, who supply countries outside the UK, visit cwr.org.uk/distributors

our Details (required for orders and donations)

ull Name:	CWR ID No. (if known):
ome Address:	
	Postcode:
elephone No. (for queries):	Email:

ublications

TITLE	QTY	PRICE	TOTAL
		Total Publications	

K P&P: up to £24.99 = **£2.99**; £25.00 and over = **FREE**

sewhere P&P: up to £10 = **£4.95**; £10.01 – £50 = **£6.95**; £50.01 – £99.99 = **£10**; £100 and over = **£30**

otal Publications and P&P (please allow 14 days for delivery)	**A**	

ubscriptions* (non direct debit)

	QTY	PRICE (including P&P)			TOTAL
		UK	Europe	Elsewhere	
very Day with Jesus (1yr, 6 issues)		£16.95	£20.95	Please contact nearest National Distributor or CWR direct	
rge Print Every Day with Jesus (1yr, 6 issues)		£16.95	£20.95		
spiring Women Every Day (1yr, 6 issues)		£16.95	£20.95		
fe Every Day (Jeff Lucas) (1yr, 6 issues)		£16.95	£20.95		
P's: 11–14s (1yr, 6 issues)		£16.95	£20.95		
pz: 7–11s (1yr, 6 issues)		£16.95	£20.95		
otal Subscriptions (subscription prices already include postage and packing)				**B**	

y use this section for subscriptions paid for by credit/debit card or cheque. For Direct Debit subscriptions see overleaf.

WR adult Bible reading notes are also available in **eBook** and **email subscription** format. Visit **cwr.org.uk** for further information.

ase circle which issue you would like your subscription to commence from:

N/FEB   MAR/APR   MAY/JUN   JUL/AUG   SEP/OCT   NOV/DEC

How would you like to hear from us?

would love to keep you up to date on all aspects of the CWR ministry, including; new lications, events & courses as well as how you can support us.

ou **DO** want to hear from us on email, please tick here [ ]

ou **DO NOT** want us to contact you by post, please tick here [ ]

Continued overleaf >>

an update your preferences at any time by contacting our customer services team on 01252 784 700. You can view our cy policy online at cwr.org.uk

Payment Details

☐ I enclose a cheque made payable to CWR for the amount of: £ _____

☐ Please charge my credit/debit card.

Cardholder's Name (in BLOCK CAPITALS) _____

Card No. ☐☐☐☐ ☐☐☐☐ ☐☐☐☐ ☐☐☐☐ ☐☐☐☐

Expires End ☐☐ ☐☐ ☐☐   Security Code ☐☐☐

Gift to CWR   ☐ Please send me an acknowledgement of my gift   C ☐

Gift Aid (your home address required, see overleaf)

giftaid it I am a UK taxpayer and want CWR to reclaim the tax on all my donations for the four years prior to thi **and on** all donations I make from the date of this Gift Aid declaration until further notice.*

Taxpayer's Full Name (in BLOCK CAPITALS) _____

Signature _____   **Date** _____

*I am a UK taxpayer and understand that if I pay less Income Tax and/or Capital Gains Tax than the amount of Gift Aid claimed on all my donations in th year it is my responsibility to pay any difference.

GRAND TOTAL (Total of A, B & C) ☐

Subscriptions by Direct Debit (UK bank account holders only)

One-year subscriptions cost £16.95 and include UK delivery. Please tick relevant boxes and fill in the form below.

☐ *Every Day with Jesus* (1yr, 6 issues)
☐ Large Print *Every Day with Jesus* (1yr, 6 issues)
☐ *Inspiring Women Every Day* (1yr, 6 issues)
☐ *Life Every Day* (Jeff Lucas) (1yr, 6 issues)

☐ *YP's*: 11–14s (1yr, 6 issues)
☐ *Topz*: 7–11s (1yr, 6 issues)

Issue to commence from
☐ Jan/Feb   ☐ Jul/Aug
☐ Mar/Apr   ☐ Sep/Oct
☐ May/Jun   ☐ Nov/Dec

CWR Instruction to your Bank or Building Society to pay by Direct Debit

Please fill in the form and send to: CWR, Waverley Abbey House, Waverley Lane, Farnham, Surrey GU9 8EP **Name and full postal address of your Bank or Building Society**

DIRE
Deb

To: The Manager   Bank/Building Society

Address _____

_____

_____

Postcode _____

Name(s) of Account Holder(s)
_____

Branch Sort Code
☐☐ ☐☐ ☐☐

Bank/Building Society Account Number
☐☐☐☐☐☐☐☐

Originator's Identification Number

4	2	0	4	8	7

Reference
☐☐☐☐☐☐☐☐☐☐☐☐☐☐☐☐☐☐

Instruction to your Bank or Building Society

Please pay CWR Direct Debits from the account detailed in this In subject to the safeguards assured by the Direct Debit Guarantee understand that this Instruction may remain with CWR and, if so, will be passed electronically to my Bank/Building Society.

Signature(s)
_____

Date _____

Banks and Building Societies may not accept Direct Debit Instructions for some types of account